cooking
moroccan

cooking
moroccan

whitecap

contents

Be enticed by a tempting array of spicy dips, glistening olives, colourful salads, grilled kebabs, crisp fried pastries and breads, all designed to whet the appetite.

Discover the aromatic dishes that are an important part of daily life in Morocco — from the street food sold at stalls in cities and towns to the family feasts served at home.

Morocco's lavish banquet food shows that its people love to celebrate with abundance, feasting on recipes that have been handed down from the palace kitchens over the centuries.

Simplicity and subtlety abound, from sweets based on fresh fruit to delicate nut-filled pastries. Refreshing drinks include sublime sharbats and mint tea, the supreme Moroccan beverage.

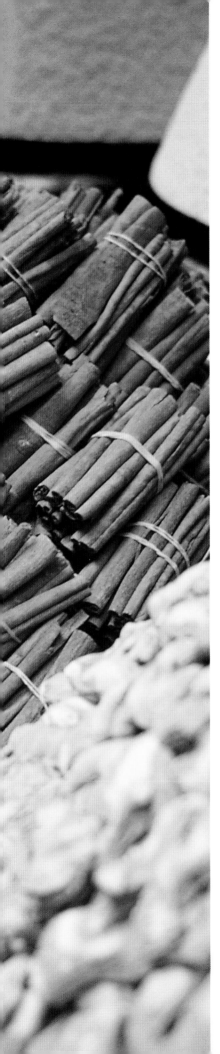

alluring aromas and flavours

The cooking of Morocco has a fascinating pedigree. While the cooking of the indigenous Berbers has always been a constant, and a basis for the creation of new recipes, its ancestry also includes Arabic, Persian and Andalusian influences. How these inputs melded and created Moroccan cuisine is a matter of history.

The Arabs spread across North Africa under the banner of Islam and, with the Berbers, invaded the Iberian Peninsula (today's Spain and Portugal) in 711, dominating the region over the next seven centuries. The invaders were known as the Moors, after the Mauri, the Berber people of Maghreb (Northwest Africa).

The Arabs named the peninsula Al Andaluz and introduced the cultivation of the saffron crocus, various citrus fruits, almonds, rice and sugar cane, as well as the use of spices, and these subsequently filtered down to Morocco. The full extent of Arabic culture, learning, medicine, cookery, architecture and agriculture took flower in Al Andaluz, mirroring that which was flourishing in the courts of the caliphs of Baghdad, who in turn had learned so much from the Persians. This was the era of the Thousand and One Arabian Nights, a time when food was extolled in poetry, and cookery books were written.

From the eleventh century to the thirteenth century, the Berber dynasties of the Almoravides and the Almohades ruled in Al Andaluz and Morocco. The lavish court kitchens of Fez, Rabat, Meknes and Marrakesh were the conduit by which new foods were introduced and recipes refined, a process that continued with later Berber dynasties.

What has evolved is a cuisine that is unique — one that makes the most of the ingredients it produces in abundance. This is evident in the dishes that use fruit for the sweet–sour flavours they impart, a Persian influence introduced via the Arabs, evolving into dishes that can only be Moroccan.

The Berbers' most important contribution to Morocco's cooking is couscous, the light and elegant grain regarded as the pasta of the Maghreb. Wheaten couscous is made into pellets with semolina grains and flour; however, cracked barley and maize are also used as a couscous.

While many of the Berber customs are maintained, such as their moussems — festivals and pilgrimages — held in vast tent cities erected for the occasion, the overriding culture is strongly intertwined with Islam. There is a strong sense of family, with all members present for the midday meal, and of hospitality, where a visitor is welcomed and given food or refreshment. During Ramadan, when Muslims fast for 30 days during the hours of daylight, and other festivals of the Muslim year, food and family are an integral part of these times of religious observance.

For any meal, there are rules to follow. Hands must be washed; at a formal gathering, a servant or young family member circulates with a jug of warm, rose-scented water, a basin and towel. On a round table, food is served in a central platter or tagine or in shallow dishes so that it can be easily picked up with the fingers. Morsels of food are picked from the communal dish with the thumb and first two fingers of the right hand and popped into the mouth, with each diner taking food from the section of the dish nearest him or her. Hands are washed again at the end of the meal before the diners retire to the reception room for mint tea and pastries.

Street food is very much part of daily life in Moroccan cities and towns. There are the ever-present kebab sellers, who grill lamb, liver or kefta (minced or ground lamb) on charcoal braziers, ready to be slipped into a wedge of Moroccan bread. In coastal cities, fish is grilled on charcoal or fried in a golden batter and presented with crisp fried eggplant (aubergine) and potato chips. Hot chickpeas are served in paper cones with a paper twist of cumin and salt. The doughnut seller with his cauldron of oil, shapes and fries crisp circles of dough.

In the cities, cafés cater to tourists, serving breakfasts of baguette or bread with butter and jam or yeast pancakes, as well as lunches such as tagines, salads, kebabs and couscous (although sandwiches and pizza are also available).

However, the best Moroccan food is that which is cooked in the home. The women are the cooks, the custodians of the recipes handed down from mother to daughter, with each cook making her own changes to suit her husband's tastes and her own. No recipe books are needed — all is memorized, to be passed on to the next generation of women. One could say that Moroccan food is a work in progress, as the modern woman does take advantage of change. Where her mother might have insisted on cooking in a tagine slaoui (the earthenware cooking pot for stews), she might work outside the home and save time by using a pressure cooker to cook the same dish. Whatever the method, the ingredients used, the resulting delectable melange of flavours and textures represents an indisputably Moroccan dish that has withstood the test of time. The recipes here aim to provide newcomers with a feel for this wonderful cuisine, exploring the ingredients, flavours and smells that are so unique to Moroccan cuisine.

little dishes

Morocco's little dishes, mukabalatt, like the antipasti of Italy, are served to whet the appetite before the main course. However, some are usually left on the table to accompany the main meal, especially the vegetables and salads. Even in the most humble household, three or four of these dishes are prepared. For a larger gathering, up to 20 different dishes are placed in the centre of the low, round table — an artist's palette of colours to entice the diners.

Spicy, jam-like dips of eggplant (aubergine) or tomato contrast with creamy white bessara, cooked vegetable salads of carrot or beetroot spiced with cumin, okra cooked in a tomato sauce, a cooked salad of wild herbs spiked with chilli and garlic, pumpkin or sweet potato cubes simmered in chermoula — the versatile, spicy, herbed mixture that is so very Moroccan. There can also be little dishes of meat and fish — small kebabs of grilled lamb and liver spiced with cumin, warm salads of brain or liver, fried stuffed sardines. Briouats, crisp fried pastries, enclose fillings of lamb, fish, prawns (shrimp) or the lemony egg and chicken filling used for bisteeya.

The distinguishing aspect of the Moroccan mukabalatt is the array of jewel-like, cooling, refreshing salads using their famous oranges, as well as carrots, luscious red tomatoes, red-skinned radishes, scarlet beetroot, crisp cucumbers and fennel bulbs, sweet or hot capsicums (peppers) and sweet red onions.

It is the combinations of these ingredients and their embellishments that set the little dishes apart, making them essentially Moroccan. A sprinkling of orange flower water here, a dusting of cinnamon or paprika there, a scattering of parsley, coriander (cilantro) or mint leaves, dates or raisins to add sweetness to the sour pieces of tangy preserved lemon rind — such transformations are made on a whim. A cucumber salad might be flavoured with a wild herb called za'atar (a Moroccan herb similar to lemon thyme, which can be used instead) and speckled with black olives, or combined with the tang of lemon juice, the sweetness of sugar and the perfume of orange flower water.

Then there are olives — little dishes of cured olives in their varied hues, unadorned or marinated in harissa, chermoula or other concoctions, glistening and inviting. And olive oil — anointing vegetables and salads where its flavour enhances and emphasizes the taste of the ingredients on the palate.

Finally, no spread of little dishes is complete without bread — used to scoop up mouthfuls of dips and shredded salads, or to soak up flavoursome dressings.

broad bean dip .... serves 6

KNOWN AS BESSARA, THIS DIP CAN ALSO BE MADE INTO A SOUP. COOK UNTIL THE BEANS ARE TENDER, PURÉE THE BEANS AND RETURN THEM TO THE PAN WITH THE REMAINING INGREDIENTS. ADD WATER TO GIVE A THICK SOUP CONSISTENCY. HEAT UNTIL BOILING AND SERVE SPRINKLED WITH CHOPPED PARSLEY, PAPRIKA AND CUMIN.

broad (fava) beans (dried or ready-skinned dried)	175 g (6 oz/1 cup)
garlic	2 cloves, crushed
ground cumin	1/2 teaspoon
lemon juice	1 1/2 tablespoons
olive oil	up to 80 ml (2 1/2 fl oz/1/3 cup)
paprika	a large pinch
flat-leaf (Italian) parsley	2 tablespoons chopped
flat bread	to serve

Put the broad beans in a bowl, cover with 500 ml (17 fl oz/2 cups) cold water and leave to soak. If using dried beans with skins, soak for 24 hours, changing the water once. If using ready-skinned dried beans, soak them for 12 hours only.

Drain the beans. If you are using beans with skins, remove the skin (slit the skin with the point of a knife and slip out the bean). Put the beans in a large saucepan with water to cover and bring to the boil. Cover and simmer over low heat for 1 hour, or until tender (if the water boils over, uncover the pan a little). Remove the lid and cook for 15 minutes, or until most of the liquid has evaporated.

Purée the beans in a food processor, then transfer to a bowl and stir in the garlic, cumin and lemon juice. Add salt, to taste. Gradually stir in enough oil to give a spreadable or thick dipping consistency. If the mixture thickens as it cools, stir through a little warm water. Spread the bean purée over a large dish and sprinkle the paprika and parsley over the top. Serve with the flat bread.

Broad beans, also known as fava beans, have been a staple food of the region for millennia — especially the dried beans, as they keep for many months. These require lengthy soaking so that the leathery skin can be removed, which results in the best flavour and a creamy white purée. Because this is time consuming, it is possible to purchase ready-skinned dried broad beans at Middle Eastern markets that only require overnight soaking. Fresh broad beans are used when in season, the young beans added to tagines with the skin on; when more mature, the beans are blanched and skinned before cooking.

marinated olives .... makes 500 g (1 lb 2 oz/3 cups)

WHEREVER OLIVES ARE SOLD, MARINATED OLIVES ARE DISPLAYED ALONGSIDE THE GREEN AND BLACK VARIETIES, WITH A LITTLE MORE ADDED TO THE PRICE TAG FOR THE EXTRA INGREDIENTS. PREPARING THEM AT HOME IS SIMPLE, WITH DELICIOUS RESULTS.

preserved lemon olives

preserved lemon	1/2
red chilli	1/2 teaspoon finely chopped
ground cumin	1/2 teaspoon
coriander (cilantro)	2 tablespoons finely chopped leaves
flat-leaf (Italian) parsley	2 tablespoons finely chopped
garlic	2 cloves, finely chopped
lemon juice	2 tablespoons
olive oil	125 ml (4 fl oz/1/2 cup)
cured green olives (whole or cracked)	500 g (1 lb 2 oz/3 cups)

harissa olives

red capsicum (pepper)	1 (or 2 tablespoons chopped roasted capsicum)
harissa	2 teaspoons
garlic	2 cloves, finely chopped
olive oil	125 ml (4 fl oz/1/2 cup)
black olives, such as Kalamata	500 g (1 lb 2 oz/2^2/3 cups)

To make the preserved lemon olives, rinse the preserved lemon under cold running water. Remove the pulp and membrane and rinse the rind. Drain and pat dry with paper towels. Chop the lemon rind very finely and place in a bowl, along with the chilli, cumin, coriander, parsley, garlic and lemon juice. Stir well and beat in the olive oil.

Rinse the green olives under cold running water and drain thoroughly. Add to the preserved lemon marinade, toss and transfer to clean jars.

To make the harissa olives, first roast the capsicum (skip this step if you have ready-prepared roasted capsicum): cut the capsicum into quarters, removing the seeds and white membrane. Have the pieces as flat as possible and place them skin side up under a hot grill (broiler) and grill (broil) until the skin blisters and blackens. Turn and cook for 2–3 minutes on the fleshy side. Place the pieces in a plastic bag, tuck the end of the bag underneath and allow to steam for 15 minutes. Remove the blackened skin, rinse and drain the capsicum pieces, then pat dry with paper towels. Finely chop one of the pieces — you will need 2 tablespoons in total. (Use the remainder in salads.) In a bowl, combine the chopped capsicum with the harissa and garlic, then beat in the olive oil.

Rinse the black olives under cold running water and drain thoroughly. Add to the harissa marinade, toss and transfer to clean jars.

Seal and refrigerate for 1–2 days before using. Bring the olives to room temperature 1 hour before serving. Use olives in the preserved lemon marinade within 5 days; the harissa-marinated olives within 10 days.

preserved lemons

Make preserved lemons with ripe, new-season fruit. The firmer the lemon, the more recently it has been picked. Store-bought lemons are usually coated with a wax, which has to be removed by scrubbing with a soft-bristle brush and warm water.

If the lemons are very firm, soak them in water for 3 days, changing the water daily. Have wide-necked sterilized jars with plastic lids on hand and wash the lemons if soaking is not required. Cut the lemons from the stem end into quarters almost to the base. Insert 1 tablespoon rock salt into each lemon, close it up and place it in a jar. Repeat until the jar is filled, sprinkling 3 teaspoons of salt between the layers. Pack the lemons into the jars as tightly as possible and add a bay leaf and a few black peppercorns to each jar if desired.

Juice more lemons and fill the jars, or add the juice of 1 lemon to each jar and fill with boiling water. Put the washed skin from a squeezed-out lemon half on top so that if any white mould forms (which is harmless), the skin and mould can be discarded when the jar is opened. Seal and store in a cool, dark place for 4 weeks, gently shaking the jars daily for the first week to dissolve the salt. The cloudy liquid clears in this time. Preserved lemons will keep for 6 months or more.

To prepare the lemons for cooking, remove a lemon from the jar with a fork. Separate the lemon into quarters and rinse it under cold running water. Remove and discard the pulp (you can add it to dishes, if you wish, but use it sparingly as it has a bitter taste). Rinse the rind, pat dry with paper towels and finely slice. Seal and refrigerate the jars once they have been opened.

lamb kebabs . . . . serves 4

WIDELY SOLD AS STREET FOOD WITH MOROCCAN BREAD, THESE SPICY LAMB KEBABS ARE ALSO OFTEN SERVED AS A LITTLE DISH. THE MEAT IS CUT INTO SMALL CUBES AND MARINATED BEFORE BEING THREADED ONTO BAMBOO OR METAL SKEWERS AND GRILLED.

boneless leg of lamb	750 g (1 lb 10 oz)
onion	1, grated
paprika	1 teaspoon
ground cumin	1 teaspoon
flat-leaf (Italian) parsley	2 tablespoons finely chopped
olive oil	60 ml (2 fl oz/$1/4$ cup)

harissa and tomato sauce

tomatoes	2
onion	$1/2$, grated to give 2 tablespoons
olive oil	1 tablespoon
harissa	1 teaspoon, or to taste (or $1/4$ teaspoon cayenne pepper)
sugar	$1/2$ teaspoon

Soak 8 bamboo skewers in water for 2 hours, or use metal skewers. Do not trim the fat from the lamb. Cut the meat into 3 cm (1$1/4$ in) cubes and put it in a bowl. Add the onion, paprika, cumin, parsley, olive oil and a generous grind of black pepper. Toss well to coat, then cover and marinate in the refrigerator for at least 2 hours.

To make the harissa and tomato sauce, halve the tomatoes horizontally and squeeze out the seeds. Coarsely grate the tomatoes into a bowl down to the skin, discarding the skin. In a saucepan, cook the onion in the olive oil for 2 minutes, stir in the harissa or cayenne pepper, and add the grated tomatoes, sugar and $1/2$ teaspoon salt. Cover and simmer for 10 minutes, then remove the lid and simmer for a further 4 minutes, or until the sauce reaches a thick, pouring consistency. Transfer to a bowl.

Thread the lamb cubes onto the skewers, leaving a little space between the meat cubes. Heat the barbecue grill to high and cook for 5–6 minutes, turning and brushing with the marinade. Alternatively, cook in a chargrill pan or under the grill (broiler).

Serve the kebabs with the sauce; alternatively, omit the sauce and serve the kebabs with separate small dishes of ground cumin and salt, to be added according to individual taste.

Leave any visible fat on the boneless leg of lamb.

Use a sharp knife to cut the lamb into large cubes.

Thread the marinated lamb cubes onto skewers.

kefta briouats .... makes 12

THESE CIGAR-SHAPED PASTRIES ARE IDEAL FOR SERVING AS APPETIZERS, PERFECT FOR PICKING UP WITH THE FINGERS. USUALLY THEY ARE FRIED, BUT WITH FILO PASTRY USED IN PLACE OF THE TRADITIONAL WARKHA PASTRY, THIS VERSION IS BAKED — MUCH EASIER TO COOK AND A GOOD DEAL HEALTHIER.

olive oil	1 tablespoon
onion	1 small, finely chopped
lean minced (ground) lamb	350 g (12 oz)
garlic	2 cloves, crushed
ground cumin	2 teaspoons
ground ginger	1/2 teaspoon
paprika	1/2 teaspoon
ground cinnamon	1/2 teaspoon
saffron threads	a pinch, soaked in a little warm water
harissa	1 teaspoon, or to taste
coriander (cilantro)	2 tablespoons chopped leaves
flat-leaf (Italian) parsley	2 tablespoons chopped
egg	1
filo pastry	6–8 sheets
butter	90 g (3 1/4 oz), melted
sesame seeds	1 tablespoon

Heat the oil in a large frying pan, add the onion and cook over low heat for 5 minutes, or until the onion is soft. Increase the heat, add the lamb and garlic and cook for 5 minutes, breaking up any lumps with the back of a wooden spoon. Add the spices, saffron water, harissa and the chopped coriander and parsley. Season to taste and cook for 1 minute, stirring to combine.

Transfer the lamb mixture to a sieve and drain to remove the fat. Put the mixture in a bowl and allow to cool slightly. Mix in the egg.

If the pastry is shorter than 39 cm (15 1/2 in) in length, you will need extra sheets. Stack on a cutting surface and, with a ruler and sharp knife, measure the length of the pastry and cut across the width to give strips 13 cm (5 in) wide and 28–30 cm (11–12 in) long. You will need 24 strips in all. Stack the filo in the folds of a dry tea towel or cover with plastic wrap to prevent it from drying out.

Put a strip of filo on a work surface with the narrow end towards you and brush with warm, melted butter. Top with another strip of filo and brush with melted butter. Put 1 tablespoon of filling 1 cm (1/2 in) in from the base and sides of the strip. Fold the end of the filo over the filling, fold in the sides and roll to the end of the strip. Place seam side down on a greased baking tray. Repeat with the remaining ingredients. Brush the rolls with melted butter and sprinkle with the sesame seeds.

Preheat the oven to 180°C (350°F/Gas 4). It is best to do this after the rolls are completed so that the kitchen remains cool during shaping. Bake the briouats for 15 minutes, or until lightly golden. Serve hot.

Brush a few pastry strips at a time with melted butter.

Put some filling on each pastry strip and roll up.

three ways with olives

OLIVES ARE OF SUCH IMPORTANCE IN THE MOROCCAN KITCHEN THAT MANY CITY STALLS AND SHOPS ARE STOCKED EXCLUSIVELY WITH THESE DELECTABLE PRESERVES. THEY ARE PICKED AT VARIOUS STAGES OF RIPENESS: GREEN AND PLUMP, PALER GREEN WITH A ROSY BLUSH, WINE RED, PURPLE BLACK, AND FINALLY BLACK AND BEGINNING TO SHRIVEL; ALL HUES MELLOW OR INTENSIFY IN THE CURING PROCESS. GREEN OLIVES ARE CRACKED BETWEEN TWO STONES TO EXPOSE THE FLESH IN CURING, AND TO ALLOW FLAVOURS TO PENETRATE IN COOKING.

cucumber and olive salad

Wash 4 Lebanese (short) cucumbers and dry with paper towels. Do not peel the cucumbers if the skin is tender. Coarsely grate the cucumbers, mix with $1/2$ teaspoon salt and leave to drain well. Add 1 finely chopped red onion and 3 teaspoons caster (superfine) sugar to the cucumber and toss together. Beat 1 tablespoon red wine vinegar with 60 ml (2 fl oz/$1/4$ cup) olive oil in a small bowl, then add 1 teaspoon finely chopped lemon thyme and freshly ground black pepper, to taste. Whisk the ingredients together and pour over the cucumber. Cover and chill for 15 minutes. Scatter with 90 g ($3^1/4$ oz/$1/2$ cup) black olives and serve with flat bread. Serves 4.

warm olives with lemon and herbs

Rinse 350 g (12 oz/2 cups) cured cracked green or black Kalamata olives, drain and place in a saucepan with enough water to cover. Bring to the boil and cook for 5 minutes, then drain in a sieve. Add 80 ml ($2^1/2$ fl oz/$1/3$ cup) olive oil and 1 teaspoon fennel seeds to the saucepan and heat until fragrant. Add 2 finely chopped garlic cloves, the drained olives, a pinch of cayenne pepper and the finely shredded zest and juice of 1 lemon. Toss for 2 minutes, or until the olives are hot. Transfer to a bowl and toss with 1 tablespoon each of finely chopped coriander (cilantro) leaves and flat-leaf (Italian) parsley. Serve hot with crusty bread to soak up the juices. Serves 4.

fennel and olive salad

Wash 2 fennel bulbs and remove the outer layers if they are wilted or damaged. Cut off the stems and slice thinly across the bulb to the base, discarding the base. Place the sliced fennel in a shallow bowl and scatter 125 g ($4^1/2$ oz/$3/4$ cup) black olives on top. Beat 2 tablespoons lemon juice with 80 ml ($2^1/2$ fl oz/$1/3$ cup) extra virgin olive oil in a jug. Season to taste and add 2 tablespoons finely chopped flat-leaf (Italian) parsley. If desired, add 1 teaspoon finely chopped, seeded red chilli. Beat well and pour over the fennel and olives just before serving. Toss lightly. Serves 4.

cucumber and olive salad

briouats with seafood .... makes 24

WHEN MAKING SMALL PASTRIES USING FILO, THE LESS THE PASTRY IS HANDLED THE BETTER. STACK THE SHEETS AND CUT THE STRIPS AS DIRECTED IN THE METHOD; A CRAFT KNIFE IS EXCELLENT FOR CUTTING THROUGH THE STACK. AVOID USING A DAMP TEA TOWEL AS IT CAN RUIN THE FILO.

filling

boneless white fish fillets	250 g (9 oz), or 200 g (7 oz) cooked, shelled prawns (shrimp)
flat-leaf (Italian) parsley	2 tablespoons finely chopped
spring onion (scallion)	1 tablespoon finely chopped
garlic	1 clove, crushed
paprika	1/2 teaspoon
ground cumin	1/4 teaspoon
cayenne pepper	a pinch
lemon juice	1 tablespoon
olive oil	1 tablespoon
filo pastry	6 sheets
egg white	1, lightly beaten
oil	for deep-frying
caster (superfine) sugar	55 g (2 oz/1/4 cup)
cayenne pepper	1/8 teaspoon
ground cinnamon	1 teaspoon

To make the filling, first poach the fish gently in lightly salted water, to cover, until the flesh flakes — about 4–5 minutes. Remove from the poaching liquid to a plate and cover closely with plastic wrap so that the surface does not dry as it cools. When cool, flake the fish. If using prawns, cut them into small pieces. Put the fish or prawns in a bowl and add the parsley, spring onion, garlic, paprika, cumin, cayenne pepper, lemon juice and olive oil and toss well to mix.

Stack the filo sheets on a cutting board, and with a ruler and sharp knife, measure and cut across the width of the pastry to give strips 13 cm (5 in) wide and 28–30 cm (11–12 in) long. You will need 24 strips. Stack the cut filo in the folds of a dry tea towel or cover it with plastic wrap to prevent it from drying out.

Take a filo strip and, with the narrow end towards you, fold it in half across its width to make a strip 6 cm (2 1/2 in) wide. Place a generous teaspoon of filling 2 cm (3/4 in) in from the base of the strip, fold the end diagonally across the filling so that the base lines up with the side of the strip, forming a triangle. Fold straight up once, then fold diagonally to the opposite side. Continue folding in this way until you near the end of the strip, then brush the filo lightly with egg white and complete the fold. Place seam side down on a cloth-covered tray. Cover with a tea towel until ready to fry. Work quickly, as the briouats are best cooked within 10 minutes of assembling.

Heat the oil to 180°C (350°F), or until a cube of bread dropped into the oil browns in 15 seconds. Add four briouats at a time and fry until golden, turning to brown evenly. Remove with a slotted spoon and drain on paper towels. Serve hot, accompanied by a small bowl of sugar mixed with cayenne and cinnamon.

Fold the pastry over the filling to form a triangle.

Brush the end of the pastry with egg white and seal the triangle.

preserved lemon and tomato salad

WITH ITS HOT CLIMATE AND FERTILE LAND, MOROCCO'S TOMATOES ARE RICHLY RED AND LUSCIOUS. THIS IS ONE OF THOSE SALADS THAT TEMPTS THE PALATE WITH ITS VARIED FLAVOURS. SERVE IT AS AN APPETIZER IN THE MOROCCAN MANNER, OR AS AN ACCOMPANIMENT TO CHARGRILLED CHICKEN OR LAMB.

tomatoes	750 g (1 lb 10 oz)
red onion	1
preserved lemon	1
olive oil	60 ml (2 fl oz/1⁄4 cup)
lemon juice	1 tablespoon
paprika	1⁄2 teaspoon
flat-leaf (Italian) parsley	1 tablespoon finely chopped
coriander (cilantro)	2 tablespoons finely chopped leaves

Peel the tomatoes. To do this, score a cross in the base of each one using a knife. Put the tomatoes in a bowl of boiling water for 20 seconds, then plunge them into a bowl of cold water to cool. Remove from the water and peel the skin away from the cross — it should slip off easily. Cut the tomatoes in half horizontally and squeeze out the seeds. Dice the tomatoes and put them in a bowl.

Halve the onion lengthways, cut out the root end, slice into slender wedges and add to the bowl.

Separate the preserved lemon into quarters, remove the pulp and membrane and discard them. Rinse the rind, pat dry with paper towels and cut into fine strips. Add to the onion and tomato.

Beat the olive oil, lemon juice and paprika, and add 1⁄2 teaspoon salt and a good grinding of black pepper. Pour over the salad, toss lightly, then cover and set aside for 30 minutes. Just before serving, add the parsley and coriander and toss again.

Taste a sun-ripened tomato plucked straight from the vine and you have an indication of the perfect Moroccan tomato. These days, store-bought tomatoes are criticized for their lack of flavour and thick skins; tomato cultivars had to be developed to withstand long trips to markets. To improve the flavour of such tomatoes, let them ripen at room temperature if necessary, store in the refrigerator, then bring to room temperature before using them in salads. If the skin is thick, remove it — there are two methods used in recipes. When used in cooking, some tomato paste (purée) and a little sugar improves the flavour.

three ways with carrots

ONE OF THE MOST POPULAR VEGETABLES FOR THE DELECTABLE APPETIZER SALADS IS THE HUMBLE CARROT. IT IS INEVITABLE THAT DISHES SHOULD REFLECT THE MOROCCANS' LOVE OF COLOUR, AND THE CARROT IS APPRECIATED FOR ITS BRILLIANT HUE AS WELL AS ITS SWEETNESS. MANY COOKS REMOVE THE CORES FROM CARROTS, ESPECIALLY WHEN CUTTING THEM INTO QUARTERS OR STICKS. INTERESTINGLY, THE ARABS INTRODUCED THE CARROT THROUGH THE MOORS TO EUROPE.

spiced carrots

Cut 500 g (1 lb 2 oz) carrots into 6 x 1.5 cm (2$\frac{1}{2}$ x $\frac{5}{8}$ in) thick sticks. Cook the carrots in boiling salted water for 10 minutes, or until tender. Drain and toss lightly with $\frac{1}{2}$ teaspoon paprika, $\frac{1}{2}$ teaspoon ground cumin, 2 tablespoons finely chopped flat-leaf (Italian) parsley, 1 tablespoon lemon juice and 2 tablespoons olive oil. Transfer to a serving bowl, cover and chill for 2 hours for the flavours to develop. Season with salt. Serve warm or at room temperature. Serves 4.

orange and carrot salad

Wash and dry 3 sweet oranges, then cut off the tops and bases. Cut the peel off using a sharp knife, removing all traces of pith and cutting through the outer membranes to expose the flesh. One at a time, hold the oranges over a bowl to catch the juice and segment them by cutting between the membranes. Remove the seeds and put the segments in the bowl. Squeeze the remains of the oranges to extract all the juice. Pour the juice into another bowl. Peel and grate 500 g (1 lb 2 oz) carrots on the shredding side of the grater or use a julienne vegetable shredder. Alternatively, julienne the carrots using a sharp knife. Put the carrots in the bowl with the orange juice and add 2 tablespoons lemon juice, 1 teaspoon ground cinnamon, 1 tablespoon caster (superfine) sugar, a small pinch of salt and 1 tablespoon orange flower water. Stir well to combine. Cover the carrot mixture and oranges and chill until required. Just before serving, drain off the accumulated juice from the oranges and arrange the segments around the edge of a serving dish. Pile the shredded carrots in the centre and top with small mint leaves. Dust the oranges lightly with a little extra cinnamon. Serves 6.

carrot soup with spices

Using the shredding side of a grater, grate 500 g (1 lb 2 oz) carrots. Place 1 grated onion in a saucepan with 30 g (1 oz) butter and cook over medium heat for 3 minutes. Add 2 crushed garlic cloves, $\frac{1}{2}$ teaspoon each of ground turmeric, ginger, cinnamon, paprika and cumin, a pinch of cayenne pepper and the grated carrot. Cook for a few seconds, then add 1.25 litres (44 fl oz/5 cups) chicken stock. Bring to the boil, cover and simmer over low heat for 15 minutes. Add 50 g (1$\frac{3}{4}$ oz/$\frac{1}{4}$ cup) couscous, stir until boiling, then cover and simmer gently for a further 20 minutes. Add 2 teaspoons lemon juice and serve hot, topped with a little chopped flat-leaf (Italian) parsley. Serves 4.

warm eggplant salad

THE INGREDIENTS OF THIS POPULAR AND TASTY MOROCCAN EGGPLANT (AUBERGINE) SALAD, CALLED ZEILOOK, ARE COOKED. THIS DELICIOUS BLEND IS IDEAL SERVED AS A DIP WITH CRUSTY BREAD. EGGPLANT HAS NEVER TASTED SO GOOD.

eggplants (aubergines)	2 x 450 g (1 lb)
tomatoes	3
olive oil	for frying
garlic	2 cloves, finely chopped
paprika	1 teaspoon
ground cumin	1/2 teaspoon
cayenne pepper	1/4 teaspoon, or to taste
coriander (cilantro)	2 tablespoons finely chopped leaves
lemon juice	2 1/2 tablespoons
preserved lemon	1/2, optional (or fresh lemon slices, to serve)

Using a vegetable peeler, remove strips of skin along the length of each eggplant. Cut the eggplants into 1 cm (1/2 in) thick slices, sprinkle with salt and layer in a colander. Leave for 20–30 minutes, then rinse under cold running water. Drain, squeeze the slices gently, then pat them dry with paper towels.

Peel the tomatoes by first scoring a cross in the base of each one using a knife. Put in a bowl of boiling water for 20 seconds, then plunge into a bowl of cold water to cool. Remove from the water and peel the skin away from the cross — it should slip off easily. Cut the tomatoes in half horizontally and squeeze out the seeds. Chop the tomatoes and set aside.

Add the olive oil to a frying pan to a depth of 5 mm (1/4 in). Heat the oil and fry the eggplant slices, in batches, until they are browned on each side. Set aside on a plate. Add more oil to the pan as needed.

Using the oil left in the pan, cook the garlic over low heat for a few seconds. Add the tomato, paprika, cumin and cayenne pepper and increase the heat to medium. Add the eggplant slices and cook, mashing the eggplant and tomato gently with a fork. Continue to cook until most of the liquid has evaporated. When the oil separates, drain off some if it seems excessive; however, some oil should be left in as it adds to the flavour of the dish. Add the coriander and lemon juice and season with freshly ground black pepper and a little salt if necessary. Tip into a serving bowl.

If using preserved lemon, rinse under cold running water and remove the pulp and membrane. Chop the rind into small pieces and scatter over the eggplant or, alternatively, garnish with slices of fresh lemon. Serve warm or at room temperature with bread.

Use a vegetable peeler to remove strips of skin from the eggplant.

stuffed sardines

SARDINES ARE AT THEIR BEST WHEN SANDWICHED WITH A FILLING OF CHERMOULA. SOME FISH MERCHANTS SPLIT AND FILLET THEM, CUTTING OFF THE TAILS, BUT IT IS EASY TO DO THIS YOURSELF AND YOU CAN EVEN LEAVE THE TAILS ON FOR EFFECT.

fresh sardines	24 whole
olive oil	for frying
plain (all-purpose) flour	for coating
lemon wedges	to serve

stuffing

onion	1 tablespoon grated and drained
garlic	1 clove, crushed
flat-leaf (Italian) parsley	3 tablespoons finely chopped
coriander (cilantro)	3 tablespoons finely chopped leaves
cayenne pepper	¼ teaspoon
paprika	½ teaspoon
freshly ground black pepper	¼ teaspoon
ground cumin	½ teaspoon
lemon zest	½ teaspoon grated
lemon juice	2 teaspoons
olive oil	2 teaspoons

To butterfly the sardines, first remove the heads. Cut through the underside of the sardines and rinse under cold running water. Snip the backbone at the tail with kitchen scissors, without cutting through the skin, and pull carefully away from the body starting from the tail end. Open out the sardines, pat the inside surface dry with paper towels and sprinkle lightly with salt. Set aside.

To make the stuffing, put the drained onion in a bowl and add the garlic, parsley, coriander, cayenne pepper, paprika, black pepper, cumin, lemon zest, lemon juice and olive oil. Mix well.

Place 12 sardines on the work surface, skin side down. Spread the stuffing evenly on each sardine and cover with another sardine, skin side up. Press them firmly together.

Add the olive oil to a large frying pan to a depth of 5 mm (¼ in) and heat. Coat the sardines with flour and fry in the hot oil for 2 minutes on each side, until crisp and evenly browned. Serve hot with lemon wedges.

Spread the stuffing over the inner side of the sardines.

Cover the stuffing with another sardine, skin side up.

Fry the flour-coated sardines in hot oil until crisp and browned.

three ways with tomatoes

THE TOMATO, ONION AND CAPSICUM SALAD HERE MAKES THE MOST OF MOROCCO'S BEAUTIFUL TOMATOES, AND IS THE MOST POPULAR SALAD SERVED IN MOROCCAN HOUSEHOLDS. THE SWEET TOMATO JAM IS A WINNING COMBINATION OF FLAVOURS, SERVED AS A DIP WITH BREAD FOR AN APPETIZER, AS A BASIS FOR A LAMB TAGINE (PAGE 77), OR USED AS A STUFFING FOR FISH. IT IS TEMPTING TO USE CANNED TOMATOES FOR THE JAM, BUT FRESH TOMATOES GIVE A SUPERIOR FLAVOUR.

okra with tomato sauce

Use 500 g (1 lb 2 oz) fresh okra, or rinse and drain 800 g (1 lb 12 oz) canned okra. Heat 60 ml (2 fl oz/¼ cup) olive oil in a large frying pan over medium heat, add 1 chopped onion and cook for 5 minutes, or until golden. Add 2 crushed garlic cloves and cook for another minute. Add the fresh okra, if using, and cook, stirring, for 4–5 minutes. Add 400 g (14 oz) can chopped tomatoes, 2 teaspoons sugar and 60 ml (2 fl oz/¼ cup) lemon juice and simmer, stirring occasionally, for 3–4 minutes. Stir in 60 g (2¼ oz/ 1½ cups) finely chopped coriander (cilantro) leaves and the canned okra, if using. Remove from the heat and serve. Serves 4–6.

tomato, onion and capsicum salad

Cut 2 green capsicums (peppers) into large flattish pieces and remove the seeds and white membrane. Place the pieces skin side up under a hot grill (broiler) and grill (broil) until the skin blackens. Turn them over and cook for 2–3 minutes on the fleshy side. Place the pieces in a plastic bag, tuck the end of the bag underneath and leave to steam in the bag until cool enough to handle. Remove the blackened skin and cut the flesh into short strips. Place in a bowl, along with 4 peeled, seeded and diced tomatoes. Halve 1 red onion lengthways, remove the root end and cut into slender wedges. Add to the bowl, along with 1 finely chopped garlic clove and 1 tablespoon finely chopped flat-leaf (Italian) parsley. Beat 80 ml (2½ fl oz/⅓ cup) olive oil with 1 tablespoon red wine vinegar and add ½ teaspoon salt and a good grinding of black pepper. Pour the dressing over the salad and toss well. Serves 4.

sweet tomato jam

Halve 1.5 kg (3 lb 5 oz) ripe tomatoes horizontally, then squeeze out the seeds. Coarsely grate the tomatoes into a bowl down to the skin, discarding the skin. Heat 60 ml (2 fl oz/¼ cup) olive oil in a heavy-based saucepan over low heat and add 2 coarsely grated onions. Cook for 5 minutes, then stir in 2 crushed garlic cloves, 1 teaspoon ground ginger, 1 cinnamon stick and ¼ teaspoon freshly ground black pepper and cook for about 1 minute. Add ¼ teaspoon ground saffron threads, if desired, 60 g (2¼ oz/¼ cup) tomato paste (purée) and the grated tomatoes and season with ½ teaspoon salt. Simmer, uncovered, over medium heat for 45–50 minutes, or until most of the liquid evaporates, stirring often when the sauce starts to thicken to prevent it catching on the base of the pan. When the oil begins to separate, stir in 2 tablespoons honey and 1½ teaspoons ground cinnamon and cook over low heat for 2 minutes. Adjust the seasoning with salt if necessary. Store in a clean, sealed jar in the refrigerator for up to 1 week. Makes 625 ml (22 fl oz/2½ cups).

okra with tomato sauce

tuna brik

THERE IS AN ART TO EATING THIS TUNISIAN SPECIALITY, ALSO POPULAR IN MOROCCO. HOLD THE BRIK BY THE CORNERS WITH THE FILLING SIDE UPWARDS AND BITE INTO THE EGG, ALLOWING THE RUNNY YOLK TO ACT AS A SAUCE FOR THE FILLING.

onion	2 tablespoons finely chopped
olive oil	2 teaspoons
anchovy fillets	3, finely chopped
canned tuna in brine	100 g (3^1/2 oz)
capers	2 teaspoons, rinsed, drained and chopped
flat-leaf (Italian) parsley	2 tablespoons finely chopped
oil	for frying
square spring roll wrappers (egg roll skins)	4 x 21 cm (8^1/2 in)
egg white	1, lightly beaten
eggs	4 small

In a small frying pan, gently cook the onion in the olive oil until softened. Add the anchovies and cook, stirring, until the anchovies have melted. Tip into a bowl. Drain the tuna well and add to the bowl, then add the capers and parsley. Mix well, breaking up the chunks of tuna.

Pour the oil into a large frying pan to a depth of 1 cm (1/2 in) and place over medium heat.

Put a spring roll wrapper on the work surface and brush the edge with beaten egg white. Put a quarter of the filling on one side of the wrapper, in a triangle shape, with the edge of the filling just touching the centre of the wrapper. Make an indent in the filling with the back of a spoon and break an egg into the centre of the filling. Fold the wrapper over to form a triangle and firmly press the edges together to seal.

As soon as you have finished the first pastry triangle, carefully lift it up using a wide spatula to help support the filling, and slide it into the hot oil. Fry for about 30 seconds on each side, spooning hot oil on top at the beginning of frying. If a firmly cooked egg is preferred, cook for 50 seconds on each side. When golden brown and crisp, remove with the spatula and drain on paper towels. Repeat with the remaining wrappers and filling. Do not be tempted to prepare all the pastry triangles before frying them, as the moist filling will soak through the wrapper.

Spread the filling on the wrapper and break an egg into the centre.

Carefully fold the wrapper over the egg to form a triangle.

Cook the pastry triangles in hot oil until golden brown and crisp.

three ways with cumin

ONE OF THE MOST-USED SPICES IN MOROCCAN COOKING, CUMIN CAN RAISE THE SIMPLEST FOODS TO NEW HEIGHTS. IT IS USED SPARINGLY IN COOKING, AND IS OFTEN SERVED AS A CONDIMENT, ESPECIALLY WITH LAMB DISHES. SMALL DISHES OF CUMIN AND SALT ARE PLACED ON THE TABLE TO BE ADDED ACCORDING TO INDIVIDUAL TASTE. STREET FOOD STALL-HOLDERS HAND OUT TWISTS OF PAPER CONTAINING CUMIN AND SALT WITH LAMB, KEFTA OR LIVER KEBABS, OR HARD-BOILED EGGS.

beetroot and cumin salad

Cut the stems from 6 medium-sized beetroots, leaving 2 cm (3/4 in) attached. Do not trim the roots. Wash well to remove all traces of soil, then boil in salted water for 1 hour, or until tender. Leave until cool enough to handle. In a deep bowl, beat 80 ml (2 1/2 fl oz/ 1/3 cup) olive oil with 1 tablespoon red wine vinegar, 1/2 teaspoon ground cumin and a good grinding of black pepper to make a dressing. Wearing rubber gloves so the beetroot juice doesn't stain your hands, peel the warm beetroot bulbs and trim the roots. Halve them and cut into slender wedges and place in the dressing. Halve 1 red onion, slice it into slender wedges and add to the beetroot. Add 2 tablespoons chopped flat-leaf (Italian) parsley and toss well. Serve warm or at room temperature. Serves 4–6.

eggplant jam

Cut 2 eggplants (aubergines), about 400 g (14 oz), into 1 cm (1/2 in) thick slices. Sprinkle with salt and drain in a colander for 30 minutes. Rinse well, squeeze gently and pat dry. Heat about 5 mm (1/4 in) of olive oil in a large frying pan over medium heat and fry the eggplant in batches until it is golden brown on both sides. Drain on paper towels, then chop finely. Put the eggplant in a colander and leave it until most of the oil has drained off, then transfer it to a bowl and add 2 crushed garlic cloves, 1 teaspoon paprika, 1 1/2 teaspoons ground cumin, 2 tablespoons chopped coriander (cilantro) leaves and 1/2 teaspoon sugar. Wipe out the pan, add the eggplant mixture and stir constantly over medium heat for 2 minutes. Transfer to a bowl, stir in 1 tablespoon lemon juice and season. Serve at room temperature. Serve with bread as a dip, or with other salads. Serves 6–8.

liver kebabs

Soak 8 bamboo skewers in water for 2 hours, or use 8 small metal skewers. Pull off the fine membrane covering a 500 g (1 lb 2 oz) piece of lamb liver. Cut the liver into 2 cm (3/4 in) thick slices, then cut into cubes, removing any tubes from the liver as necessary. Put in a bowl and sprinkle with 1 teaspoon paprika, 1/2 teaspoon ground cumin, 1/4 teaspoon cayenne pepper and 1 teaspoon salt. Add 2 tablespoons olive oil and toss well. Set aside for 5 minutes. Thread 5 or 6 pieces of liver onto each skewer, leaving a little space between the pieces. Cook on a barbecue grill or in a chargrill pan, brushing with any of the oil remaining in the bowl. Cook for about 1 minute each side — the liver should remain pink in the centre, otherwise it will toughen. Serve the kebabs with 1 round of Moroccan bread or pitta breads. If using Moroccan bread, cut the bread into quarters and slit each piece in half almost to the crust. For each serve, slide the liver from 2 skewers into the bread pocket. If using pitta bread, do not split it; just slide the liver from the skewers onto the centre and fold up the sides. Offer small separate dishes of ground cumin, coarse salt and cayenne pepper to be added to taste, or stir 60 ml (2 fl oz/1/4 cup) hot water into 3 tablespoons harissa and serve as a sauce. Serves 4.

beetroot and cumin salad

merguez with
capsicum and onion .... serves 4

CHARGRILLED MERGUEZ SAUSAGE SERVED WITH FLAT MOROCCAN BREAD, FRIED CAPSICUM (PEPPER) AND ONION
IS ONE OF THE DELIGHTS OF MOROCCAN STREET FOOD STALLS. IT IS ALSO SERVED AS AN APPETIZER — CUT THE
COOKED SAUSAGE INTO BITE-SIZED PIECES, MIX WITH THE VEGETABLES AND SERVE IT IN A SHALLOW BOWL.

merguez sausages	8
green capsicums (peppers)	2
red capsicum (pepper)	1
onion	1 large
olive oil	2 tablespoons
Moroccan bread	2 rounds (or pitta breads, to serve)

Prick the sausages with a fork, then cook on a barbecue grill over low to medium heat, turning frequently until cooked through — this will take about 8–10 minutes. Alternatively, cook the sausages in a chargrill pan.

Meanwhile, cut the capsicums into quarters, remove the seeds and white membrane and cut into strips about 1 cm (1/2 in) wide. Halve the onion and slice thinly. Heat the olive oil in a frying pan on the barbecue, add the capsicum strips and onion and cook over medium heat, stirring often, for about 10 minutes, or until tender. If the onion begins to burn, reduce the heat to low or move the pan to a cooler section of the barbecue. Season with salt and freshly ground black pepper.

If serving with Moroccan bread, cut the rounds into quarters. Put the sausages and a generous amount of the capsicum mixture in the bread or roll up in pitta bread. Alternatively, serve the sausages on plates with the vegetables, and the bread on the side.

Fiery hot merguez sausage is a Tunisian speciality adopted by Moroccans, although their version is not as hot as the original. Made of lamb with a fair portion of lamb fat to give it moistness and succulence, it is hot and pungent with the addition of harissa (hot chilli paste) and garlic, and flavoured with ground fennel and coriander seeds, cumin, paprika, black pepper and allspice. Gourmet butchers and delicatessens, as well as some Middle Eastern food markets, stock merguez. Traditionally a thin sausage, its length can vary.

the bakery

To a Moroccan, bread, or khobz, is sacred, to be revered, savoured and never wasted. Kesra, or country bread, is made every day in rural households, the dough mixed and kneaded in a shallow wooden or earthenware vessel called a gsaa. It is a simple bread, made with wholemeal (whole wheat) flour, usually mixed with unbleached flour, and perhaps a handful of yellow cornmeal or barley flour. Only water, a little salt and sugar are used in the dough, which is leavened with a sourdough starter kept from the previous day's baking (though often supplemented with dried yeast granules these days).

Shaped in flattish round loaves and placed on trays, the loaves are stamped with each household's own mark for identification, covered with a cloth and left to rise only once. Anise seeds and sesame seeds are sometimes used to flavour the bread, or are sprinkled over the top. The loaves are then taken on trays to the local bakery or baked in a communal oven — the marking on each loaf clearly identifying the owner.

These flattish loaves have a loose crumb that can absorb the sauce of the tagine, but are still crusty enough to support food as it is conveyed to the mouth with the fingers. The bread is cut into wedges and distributed by one person at the table — to prevent household quarrels. Flatter loaves are made for eating with kebabs, and baguettes, a legacy from the French, are baked in some bakeries and patisseries.

Other breads of the bled, or countryside, include a bread sheet called therfist, which is cooked on a pottery dome over embers. Another, made by the Tuaregs, the nomadic Berbers of the Sahara, is called tagella and is cooked on hot stones.

filled savoury pancakes .... makes 12

THESE YEAST-DOUGH PANCAKES ARE FLAKY, LIGHT AND CRISP AS A RESULT OF CAREFUL ROLLING AND FOLDING. THE SPICED KEFTA MIXTURE IS A SUBSTITUTE FOR A PRESERVED SPICED MEAT CALLED KHLII, TRADITIONALLY USED IN MOROCCO FOR THESE DELICIOUS SNACK BREADS.

active dried yeast	2 teaspoons
sugar	1 teaspoon
plain (all-purpose) flour	350 g (12 oz/2¾ cups)
olive oil	for coating
oil	for frying

spiced kefta paste

smen or ghee	4 tablespoons
finely minced (ground) beef	250 g (9 oz)
onion	2 tablespoons grated
garlic	4 cloves, finely chopped
ground cumin	2 teaspoons
ground coriander	2 teaspoons

Dissolve the yeast in 125 ml (4 fl oz/½ cup) lukewarm water and stir in the sugar. Sift the flour and ½ teaspoon salt into a shallow bowl and make a well in the centre. Pour the yeast mixture into the well, then add another 125 ml (4 fl oz/½ cup) lukewarm water. Stir sufficient flour into the liquid to form a thin batter, cover the bowl with a cloth and leave for 15 minutes until bubbles form. Gradually stir in the remaining flour, then mix with your hand until a sticky dough is formed. If it is too stiff, add a little more water. Knead for 10 minutes in the bowl until smooth and elastic. Pour a little olive oil down the side of the bowl, turn the ball of dough to coat in the oil, cover and leave in a warm place for 30 minutes.

To make the spiced kefta, heat the smen or ghee in a frying pan, add the beef and stir over high heat until browned. Reduce the heat to low, add the onion, garlic, cumin and coriander and season with salt and freshly ground black pepper. Cook, stirring, for 2 minutes, then add 500 ml (17 fl oz/2 cups) water. Cover and simmer for 30–45 minutes until the water evaporates and the fat separates. Tip into a food processor and process to a paste; alternatively, pound to a paste in a mortar. Set aside to cool.

Using oiled hands, punch down the dough and divide into 12 balls. Oil the work surface and the rolling pin and roll out and stretch a dough ball into an 18 cm (7 in) circle. Spread thinly with a tablespoon of kefta paste. Fold the sides in so that they overlap, then fold in the other two sides to overlap in the centre. Roll out and shape into a 9 x 13 cm (3½ x 5 in) rectangle. Place on an oiled tray and repeat with the remaining ingredients.

In a frying pan, add the oil to a depth of 1 cm (½ in). Place over high heat and, when almost smoking, reduce the heat to medium and add two pancakes. Cook for about 1 minute on each side, or until browned and crisp and cooked through. Drain on paper towels and repeat with the remaining pancakes. Serve hot.

Roll out and stretch each portion of dough into a circle.

Fold the sides of the dough over the kefta paste.

moroccan bread .... makes 3 loaves

STORE ACTIVE DRIED YEAST IN THE REFRIGERATOR. IF PAST ITS USE-BY DATE, DISSOLVE ½ TEASPOON EACH OF THE YEAST AND SUGAR IN 3 TABLESPOONS WARM WATER AND LEAVE FOR 15 MINUTES. IF IT FROTHS, USE THE YEAST, OTHERWISE DISCARD IT AND PURCHASE A NEW BATCH.

active dried yeast	3 teaspoons
bread flour or plain (all-purpose) flour, preferably unbleached	500 g (1 lb 2 oz/4 cups)
wholemeal (whole wheat) flour	200 g (7 oz/1⅓ cups)
milk	125 ml (4 fl oz/½ cup) lukewarm
cornmeal or polenta	2 tablespoons
whole aniseed, roasted sesame seeds, black sesame seeds or coarse salt	1 tablespoon, optional

Dissolve the yeast in 125 ml (4 fl oz/½ cup) lukewarm water. Sift the flours and 1½ teaspoons salt into a mixing bowl and make a well in the centre. Pour the yeast mixture into the well, then add another 250 ml (9 fl oz/1 cup) lukewarm water and the lukewarm milk. Stir sufficient flour into the liquid to form a thin batter, cover the bowl with a cloth and leave for 15 minutes until bubbles form.

Gradually stir in the remaining flour, then mix with your hand to form a soft dough, adding a little extra water if necessary. Turn out onto a lightly floured work surface and knead for 10 minutes until smooth and elastic and the dough springs back when an impression is made with a finger. Only knead in extra plain flour if the dough remains sticky after a few minutes of kneading.

As the dough requires only one rising, divide it into three even-sized pieces. Shape each piece into a ball and roll out on a lightly floured work surface to rounds 23 cm (9 in) in diameter or 26 cm (10½ in) for flatter breads.

Sift the cornmeal or polenta onto baking trays. Lift the rounds onto the trays, reshaping if necessary. Brush the tops lightly with water and, if desired, sprinkle with any one of the toppings, pressing it in lightly. Cover the loaves with tea towels and leave in a warm, draught-free place for 1 hour to rise. The bread has risen sufficiently when a depression remains in the dough after it is pressed lightly with a fingertip.

While the loaves are rising, preheat the oven to 220°C (425°F/Gas 7). Just before baking, prick the breads in several places with a fork. Put the breads in the hot oven and bake for 12–15 minutes, or until they are golden and sound hollow when the base is tapped. Cool on a wire rack. Cut in wedges to serve. Use on the day of baking. Any leftover loaves may be frozen.

Knead the dough on a floured surface until smooth and elastic.

Lift the dough onto a tray and reshape if necessary.

a simple feast

Where there is lamb grilling over charcoal fires, aromas assail the senses. Moroccan bread, filled with tender cubes redolent with spices, is very inviting indeed. A simple feast, so typical of the street food that is served by the many stalls found in city squares and souks. The two most popular soups, harira and bessara, are ladled out of simmering cauldrons into pottery bowls. In the evenings, long tables laden with salads, tagines and couscous tempt customers, who sit on benches and are served by white-garbed men.

In their homes, Moroccan women also prepare their own delicious meals. Using the most basic kitchen equipment, they have developed the cuisine to its present form. They cook with confidence — a pinch of this, a handful of that — just as their mothers have taught them, adding and changing according to their own family's preferences.

Onions, garlic, fresh herbs and spices are staples of Moroccan cuisine, and lamb, chicken, chickpeas and lentils are always available. However, the choice of vegetables and fruits added to tagines and stews is dictated by the seasons. In spring, tender young broad (fava) beans can be cooked whole or shelled, but they will need to be skinned as well when more mature. Spring to early summer is the time for fresh green peas, green beans, zucchini (courgettes), wild artichokes and eggplants (aubergines). Tomatoes, cucumbers and capsicums (peppers) are at their best in summer, with autumn heralding the arrival of turnips, quinces, the best oranges, apples and pears. Beetroot, cauliflower, celery and fennel bulbs are winter fare. Pumpkin (winter squash) mature in winter but keep well. Stone fruits, melons and berries abound in summer, with other produce available year-round.

The woman of the household prepares the main meal, served at midday, and it is a family feast. Usually it features a tagine of lamb or chicken extended with the addition of chickpeas — or it could be a tagine of chickpeas or lentils; if it is Friday, couscous is cooked. The day's choice of vegetables and fruits dictate what is put in the tagine and which salad and vegetable dishes will be prepared. Cooking could be over a charcoal brazier or a flame from a gas bottle, although gas cookers are increasingly replacing traditional methods. With the day's bread having been made and baked in the morning, the meal is complete. Fresh fruit is served at the end of the meal, followed by mint tea and perhaps a simple sweet biscuit.

chicken soup with couscous

USE A WHOLE CHICKEN SUITABLE FOR STEWING AND CUT IT INTO QUARTERS, OR USE CHICKEN PIECES FOR CONVENIENCE. WHEN COOKED, THE CHICKEN MUST BE TENDER ENOUGH FOR THE MEAT TO BE EASILY REMOVED FROM THE BONES.

chicken	1.5 kg (3 lb 5 oz), quartered
olive oil	2 tablespoons
onions	2, finely chopped
ground cumin	1/2 teaspoon
paprika	1/2 teaspoon
harissa	1/2 teaspoon, or to taste (or 1/4 teaspoon cayenne pepper)
tomatoes	2
tomato paste (purée)	1 tablespoon
sugar	1 teaspoon
cinnamon stick	1
couscous	100 g (3 1/2 oz/1/2 cup)
flat-leaf (Italian) parsley	2 tablespoons finely chopped
coriander (cilantro)	1 tablespoon finely chopped leaves
dried mint	1 teaspoon
lemon wedges	to serve

Remove and discard the skin from the chicken. Heat the olive oil in a large saucepan or stockpot, add the chicken and cook over high heat for 2–3 minutes, stirring often. Reduce the heat to medium, add the onion and cook for 5 minutes, or until the onion has softened. Stir in the cumin, paprika and harissa or cayenne pepper. Add 1 litre (35 fl oz/4 cups) water and bring to the boil.

Halve the tomatoes horizontally and squeeze out the seeds. Coarsely grate the tomatoes over a plate down to the skin, discarding the skin. Add the grated tomato to the pot, along with the tomato paste, sugar, cinnamon stick, 1 teaspoon salt and some freshly ground black pepper. Bring to the boil, reduce the heat to low, then cover and simmer for 1 hour, or until the chicken is very tender.

Remove the chicken to a dish using a slotted spoon. When it is cool enough to handle, remove the bones and tear the chicken meat into strips. Return the chicken to the pot with an additional 500 ml (17 fl oz/2 cups) water and return to the boil. While it is boiling, gradually pour in the couscous, stirring constantly. Reduce the heat, then stir in the parsley, coriander and mint and simmer, uncovered, for 20 minutes. Adjust the seasoning and serve with lemon wedges to squeeze over, and crusty bread.

Cut the tomatoes in half and squeeze out the seeds.

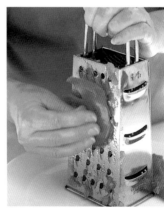

Grate the tomatoes down to the skin, then discard the skin.

kefta kebabs

THESE DELICIOUS SAUSAGE-SHAPED KEBABS ARE SOLD AS STREET FOOD IN MOROCCO, SERVED IN WEDGES OF MOROCCAN BREAD WITH A FIERY HARISSA AND TOMATO SAUCE (PAGE 21). THEY ARE ALSO MADE INTO SMALL, ROUND PATTIES AND CHARGRILLED.

onion	1 small, roughly chopped
flat-leaf (Italian) parsley	2 tablespoons chopped
coriander (cilantro)	1 tablespoon chopped leaves
minced (ground) lamb or beef	500 g (1 lb 2 oz)
ground cumin	1 teaspoon
paprika	1 teaspoon
cayenne pepper	1/4 teaspoon
freshly ground black pepper	1/4 teaspoon
salad greens	to serve
lemon wedges	to serve

Put the onion, parsley and coriander in a food processor and process to a purée. Add the lamb or beef, cumin, paprika, cayenne pepper, black pepper and 1 teaspoon salt. Process to a paste, scraping the side of the bowl occasionally.

Divide the kefta mixture into eight even portions. Moisten your hands with water and mould each portion into a sausage shape about 9 cm (3 1/2 in) long. Place on a tray, cover with plastic wrap and chill for 1 hour.

Insert a flat metal skewer through the centre of each kefta sausage. Cook on a hot barbecue grill or in a chargrill pan, turning frequently to brown evenly. The kefta are cooked until they are just well done (about 10 minutes) — they will feel firm when pressed lightly with tongs.

Serve the keftas with salad greens and lemon wedges. If desired, provide separate small dishes of ground cumin and salt, to be added according to individual taste.

Mould each portion of the kefta mixture into a sausage shape.

Insert a metal skewer through each kefta sausage.

spicy blends

Harissa (pictured below) is a hot and spicy Tunisian condiment that the Moroccans have adopted and adapted to their tastes. To make it, roughly chop 125 g (4½ oz) dried red chillies and soak in boiling water for 1 hour. Drain the chillies and put them in a food processor with 10 chopped garlic cloves, 1 tablespoon each of mint, ground coriander and ground cumin, 1 teaspoon ground caraway seeds, 1 tablespoon olive oil and ½ teaspoon salt. Process to a purée. With the motor running, gradually add another 100 ml (3½ fl oz) olive oil, scraping the side of the bowl when necessary. Spoon the thick paste into a 600 ml (21 fl oz) sterilized jar. Cover the top of the harissa with a thin layer of olive oil and seal the jar. Store in the refrigerator for up to 6 months. Harissa is also available at gourmet food stores and Middle Eastern markets. Use it with caution as it is very hot.

Chermoula is a marinade and sauce indispensable for fish cookery, and can also serve as a marinade for poultry and lamb. It is an inspired blend of ingredients — coriander (cilantro), flat-leaf (Italian) parsley, garlic, onion, cumin, ground coriander, saffron, paprika and cayenne pepper. There are many versions of this typically Moroccan marinade, with the ingredients varying depending on the cook or the food it is to partner. Preserved lemon rind, lemon juice or vinegar are sometimes added. Olive oil is essential.

spiced grilled chicken . . . . serves 4

THE MOROCCAN SPICES AND SUGAR-DIPPED, GRILLED LEMON QUARTERS ADD AN EXOTIC TOUCH TO BARBECUED CHICKEN. WARM PUMPKIN SALAD WITH PRESERVED LEMON (PAGE 86) GOES WELL AS AN ACCOMPANIMENT AND CAN BE COOKED ON THE BARBECUE ALONGSIDE THE CHICKEN.

chickens	2 x 750 g (1 lb 10 oz)
saffron threads	a pinch
coarse salt	1 teaspoon
garlic	2 cloves, chopped
paprika	1 1/2 teaspoons
cayenne pepper	1/4 teaspoon
ground cumin	2 teaspoons
freshly ground black pepper	1/2 teaspoon
lemon juice	1 tablespoon
olive oil	1 tablespoon
lemons	2
icing (confectioners') sugar	2 tablespoons
watercress	to serve

To prepare the chickens, cut them on each side of the backbone using poultry shears or kitchen scissors. Rinse the chickens and dry with paper towels. Open out on a board, skin side up, and press down with the heel of your hand on the top of each breast to break the breastbone and to flatten it. Cut deep slashes diagonally in each breast and on the legs. Push 4 long metal skewers from the tip of each breast through to the underside of the legs, which should be spread outwards so that the thickness of the chicken is as even as possible.

Put the saffron in a mortar with the salt and pound with a pestle to pulverize the threads. Add the garlic and pound to a paste. Work in the paprika, cayenne pepper, cumin, black pepper, lemon juice and olive oil. Rub the spice mix into the chickens, rubbing it into the slashes. Cover and marinate in the refrigerator for at least 2 hours, or overnight. Bring the chickens to room temperature 1 hour before cooking.

Prepare a charcoal fire or preheat the barbecue and place the chickens on the grill, skin side up. Cook over medium heat for 20 minutes, continually turning the chicken as it cooks and brushing with any remaining marinade. The chicken is cooked if the juices run clear when the thigh is pierced with a knife. Cooking time can be shortened on a barbecue if a roasting tin is inverted over the chickens to act as a mini oven — reduce the heat to low to prevent burning. Transfer the chickens to a platter, remove the skewers, cover with a foil tent and leave to rest for 5 minutes before cutting in half to serve.

Cut the lemons in half horizontally, remove any seeds, then cut again into quarters. Sift the icing sugar onto a large plate. Dip the cut surfaces of the lemon quarters in the icing sugar and place on the barbecue hotplate. Cook briefly on the cut surfaces until golden and caramelized. Serve the chickens with the lemon wedges and watercress.

Press down on each chicken breast to flatten it.

Push skewers from the breast to the underside of the legs.

steamed lamb with cumin . . . . serves 4

THIS IS A DISH OF SIMPLE BUT DELICIOUS FLAVOURS. WHEN SERVED AS PART OF A MOROCCAN MEAL, MORSELS OF LAMB ARE GENTLY PULLED FROM THE BONE WITH THE FINGERS. HOWEVER, THE LAMB CAN BE SLICED AND SERVED WITH BEETROOT AND CUMIN SALAD (PAGE 41) AND TINY BOILED POTATOES.

lamb shoulder on the bone	1.25 kg (2 lb 12 oz)
ground cumin	1 1/2 teaspoons, plus extra, to serve
coarse salt	1 teaspoon, plus extra, to serve
freshly ground black pepper	1/2 teaspoon
ground saffron threads	a pinch
garlic	6 cloves, bruised
parsley	10–12 stalks
olive oil	1 tablespoon

Trim the excess fat from the whole shoulder of lamb if necessary. Wipe the meat with damp paper towels and then cut small incisions into the meat on each side.

Combine the cumin, salt, black pepper and saffron and rub the mixture into the lamb, pushing it into the incisions. Cover and leave for 30 minutes for the flavours to penetrate. Place the lamb fat side up on a piece of muslin, top with half the garlic cloves and tie the muslin over the top.

Using a large saucepan onto which a steamer will fit, or the base of a couscoussier, fill it three-quarters full with water. If using a saucepan and steamer, check that the base of the steamer is at least 3 cm (1 1/4 in) above the surface of the water. Cover the pan and bring to the boil. Line the base of the steamer with the parsley stalks and the remaining garlic cloves. Place the lamb on top, put folded strips of foil around the rim of the steamer and put the lid on firmly to contain the steam. Keeping the heat just high enough to maintain a boil, steam the lamb for 2–2 1/2 hours — do not lift the lid for the first 1 1/2 hours of cooking. The lamb should easily pull away from the bone when cooked. Lift it out of the steamer and remove the muslin.

Heat the olive oil in a large frying pan and quickly brown the lamb on each side for a more attractive presentation. Serve with little dishes of coarse salt and ground cumin, if desired.

Rub the spice mixture into the lamb, pushing it into the incisions.

Wrap a piece of muslin around the lamb and tie it together.

three ways with chermoula

THIS HERB AND SPICE MIX IS A MOROCCAN SPECIALITY PARTICULARLY SUITED TO SEAFOOD. THE SPICY PRAWNS (SHRIMP) GIVE A VERSION OF CHERMOULA WITH THE EMPHASIS ON SPICES, WHILE THE OTHERS FEATURE HERBS. THE CHERMOULA CAN BE STORED IN A SEALED JAR IN THE REFRIGERATOR FOR UP TO 3 DAYS. USE IT AS A MARINADE AND BASTE FOR BARBECUED OR CHARGRILLED FISH, CALAMARI OR BABY OCTOPUS, BUT ONLY MARINATE FISH FOR 5 MINUTES AS THE LEMON JUICE COULD 'COOK' IT.

prawns in chermoula

Peel 1 kg (2 lb 4 oz) raw large prawns (shrimp), leaving the tails intact. To devein the prawns, cut a slit down the back and remove any visible vein. Place the prawns in a colander and rinse under cold running water. Shake the colander to remove any excess water, sprinkle the prawns with 1/2 teaspoon salt, toss through and set aside. To make the chermoula, remove the pulp from 1/2 preserved lemon, rinse the rind and pat dry. Roughly chop and place in a food processor, along with 2 roughly chopped garlic cloves, 3 tablespoons each of chopped flat-leaf (Italian) parsley and chopped coriander (cilantro) leaves, 2 tablespoons lemon juice, 1/4 teaspoon ground saffron threads, if desired, 1/2 teaspoon each of paprika and ground cumin and 1/8–1/4 teaspoon cayenne pepper, to taste. Process to a coarse paste, gradually adding 60 ml (2 fl oz/1/4 cup) olive oil while processing. Heat 2 tablespoons olive oil in a large frying pan over medium to high heat, then add the prawns and cook, stirring often, until they begin to turn pink. Reduce the heat to medium, add the chermoula and continue to cook, stirring often, for 3 minutes, or until the prawns are firm. Serve hot with lemon wedges and saffron rice (page 135). Serves 4.

spicy prawns

Prepare, rinse and drain 375 g (13 oz) raw medium prawns (shrimp) as described above. Pour 60 ml (2 fl oz/1/4 cup) olive oil into a large frying pan and place over medium heat. Stir in 1/2 teaspoon ground cumin, 1/2 teaspoon cumin seeds, 1 teaspoon ground ginger and 2 teaspoons chopped red chilli. Cook until fragrant and the cumin seeds start to pop, then add 3 finely chopped garlic cloves, 1/2 teaspoon ground turmeric and 1 teaspoon paprika. Cook, stirring for a few seconds, then add the prawns. Increase the heat a little and fry the prawns, tossing frequently, for 3–4 minutes until they firm up and turn pink. Stir in 2 tablespoons finely chopped coriander (cilantro) leaves and 60 ml (2 fl oz/1/4 cup) water, bring to a simmer and remove from the heat. Serve immediately with lemon wedges. Serves 4 as an appetizer.

tuna skewers with chermoula

Soak 8 bamboo skewers in water for 2 hours, or use 8 metal skewers. Cut 800 g (1 lb 12 oz) tuna steaks into 3 cm (1 1/4 in) cubes. Put the tuna in a shallow non-metallic dish. Combine 2 tablespoons olive oil, 1/2 teaspoon ground cumin and 2 teaspoons finely grated lemon zest and pour over the tuna. Toss to coat, then cover and chill for 10 minutes. To make the chermoula, cook 1/2 teaspoon ground coriander, 1 1/2 teaspoons each of ground cumin and paprika and a pinch of cayenne pepper in a frying pan over medium heat until fragrant. Tip into a bowl, add 3 crushed garlic cloves, 3 tablespoons each of chopped flat-leaf (Italian) parsley and chopped coriander (cilantro) leaves and 60 ml (2 fl oz/1/4 cup) each of lemon juice and olive oil and stir through. Thread the tuna onto the skewers. Lightly oil a chargrill pan or barbecue grill and cook the skewers for 1 minute on each side for rare, or 2 minutes for medium, or until cooked to taste. Serve drizzled with the chermoula. Serves 4.

prawns in chermoula

fish soup

serves 6

WITH SUCH A VARIETY OF FISH AVAILABLE, IT IS SURPRISING THAT THERE ARE SO FEW FISH SOUP RECIPES IN MOROCCAN COOKING. THIS SOUP IS TYPICAL OF THE CUISINE IN TETUÁN, IN THE COUNTRY'S NORTH, WHERE SPANISH INFLUENCES STILL PREVAIL.

red capsicums (peppers)	2
long red chilli	1
extra virgin olive oil	2 tablespoons
onion	1, finely chopped
tomato paste (purée)	1 tablespoon
harissa	2–3 teaspoons, to taste
garlic	4 cloves, finely chopped
ground cumin	2 teaspoons
fish stock	750 ml (26 fl oz/3 cups)
crushed tomatoes	400 g (14 oz) can
firm white fish, such as	750 g (1 lb 10 oz), cut into 2 cm
blue eye cod or ling	(³/4 in) cubes
bay leaves	2
coriander (cilantro)	2 tablespoons chopped leaves

Cut the capsicums into quarters and remove the membrane and seeds. Cut the chilli in half and remove the seeds. Place the capsicum and chilli skin side up under a hot grill (broiler) and grill (broil) until the skin blackens. Remove and place in a plastic bag, tuck the end of the bag underneath and leave to steam until cool enough to handle. Remove the skin, cut the flesh into thin strips and reserve.

Heat the oil in a large saucepan and cook the onion for 5 minutes, or until softened. Stir in the tomato paste, harissa, garlic, cumin and 125 ml (4 fl oz/¹/2 cup) water. Add the stock, tomatoes and 500 ml (17 fl oz/2 cups) water. Bring to the boil, then reduce the heat and add the fish and bay leaves. Simmer for 7–8 minutes.

Remove the fish and discard the bay leaves. When the soup has cooled slightly, add half the coriander and purée until smooth. Season with salt and pepper. Return the soup to the pan, add the fish, capsicum and chilli and simmer gently for 5 minutes. Garnish with the remaining coriander and serve hot with crusty bread.

Used from antiquity in the Middle East, cumin was introduced into Morocco by the Arabs and has become one of the most popular spices, used in fish and chicken tagines and soups, and mixed with salt and sprinkled on kebabs and hard-boiled eggs. It is essential for mechoui (slow-roasted lamb). Many Moroccan cooks prefer to freshly pound cumin seeds to attain maximum flavour. A darker cumin — greenish-brown in colour — is the one to choose, as lighter cumin could be mixed with ground coriander seeds. It should have an oily feel between the fingers with a warm and sweet, yet pungent and earthy, aroma.

saffron fish balls in tomato sauce

THIS RECIPE WAS DEVISED BY MOROCCAN JEWS, WHO WERE ALSO THE PRINCIPAL GATHERERS OF THE SAFFRON CROCUS WHEN IT WAS INTRODUCED FROM MOORISH SPAIN. IT IS BASED ON THEIR TRADITIONAL RECIPE FOR FISH BALLS, BUT WITH DISTINCTIVE MOROCCAN FLAVOURS. ANY WHITE FISH FILLETS CAN BE USED.

boneless white fish fillets	500 g (1 lb 2 oz)
egg	1
spring onions (scallions)	2, chopped
flat-leaf (Italian) parsley	1 tablespoon chopped
coriander (cilantro)	1 tablespoon chopped leaves
fresh breadcrumbs	55 g (2 oz/^{2}/$_3$ cup)
ground saffron threads	^{1}/$_8$ teaspoon

tomato sauce

tomatoes	500 g (1 lb 2 oz)
onion	1, coarsely grated
olive oil	60 ml (2 fl oz/^{1}/$_4$ cup)
garlic	2 cloves, finely chopped
paprika	1 teaspoon
harissa	^{1}/$_2$ teaspoon, or to taste (or ^{1}/$_4$ teaspoon cayenne pepper)
ground cumin	^{1}/$_2$ teaspoon
sugar	1 teaspoon

Cut the fish fillets into rough pieces and put in a food processor, along with the egg, spring onion, parsley, coriander and breadcrumbs. Mix the saffron with 1 tablespoon warm water and add to the other ingredients with ^{3}/$_4$ teaspoon salt and some freshly ground black pepper. Process to a thick paste, scraping down the side of the bowl occasionally.

With moistened hands, shape the fish mixture into balls the size of a walnut. Put on a tray, cover and set aside in the refrigerator.

To make the tomato sauce, first peel the tomatoes by scoring a cross in the base of each one using a knife. Put them in a bowl of boiling water for 20 seconds, then plunge them into a bowl of cold water to cool. Remove from the water and peel the skin away from the cross — it should slip off easily. Halve the tomatoes horizontally and squeeze out the seeds. Chop the tomatoes and set aside.

Put the onion and olive oil in a saucepan and cook over medium heat for 5 minutes. Add the garlic, paprika, harissa or cayenne pepper and cumin. Stir for a few seconds, then add the chopped tomato, sugar, 250 ml (9 fl oz/1 cup) water and salt and freshly ground black pepper, to taste. Bring to the boil, cover and simmer for 15 minutes.

Add the fish balls to the tomato sauce, shaking the pan occasionally as they are added so that they settle into the sauce. Return to a gentle boil over medium heat, then cover and reduce the heat to low. Simmer for 20 minutes. Serve the fish balls hot with crusty bread.

Shape the fish mixture into balls the size of a walnut.

Peel the tomato skin away from the cross.

three ways with chickpeas

THE CHICKPEA HAS BEEN USED AS A FOOD IN THE MEDITERRANEAN REGION SINCE ANCIENT TIMES. IN MOROCCO, WHERE OFTEN ONLY A SMALL AMOUNT OF MEAT AND CHICKEN OFF-CUTS ARE USED IN A DISH, CHICKPEAS ADD SUBSTANCE AND NUTRITIONAL VALUE. MOROCCAN COOKS USUALLY SKIN THE CHICKPEAS WHEN ADDING THEM TO TAGINES (SEE PAGE 110), BUT NOT FOR SOUPS OR FOR STREET FOOD AS IN THE FOLLOWING RECIPE FOR HOT CHICKPEAS. THESE CHICKPEAS ARE DRAINED OF EXCESS LIQUID AFTER COOKING, AND SERVED IN PAPER CONES.

hot chickpeas

Use either 225 g (8 oz/1 cup) dried chickpeas or 2 x 425 g (15 oz) cans chickpeas. To cook dried chickpeas, soak them overnight in three times their volume of cold water. Drain and place in a saucepan with fresh water to cover and simmer gently for 1 hour, or until tender, adding salt to taste towards the end of cooking. Drain, reserving 250 ml (9 fl oz/1 cup) of the cooking liquid. If using canned chickpeas, drain them, reserving 250 ml (9 fl oz/1 cup) of the liquid. Warm 2 tablespoons olive oil in a saucepan over medium heat. Add 1 finely chopped onion and cook until lightly golden, then add 1 chopped small green capsicum (pepper), 1 teaspoon ground cumin and 2 tablespoons finely chopped coriander (cilantro) leaves and cook for a few seconds. Add the chickpeas and their liquid, and freshly ground black pepper, to taste. Bring to a simmer, cover and simmer until heated through. Adjust the seasoning and serve hot in small bowls with bread. Serves 4–6.

tagine of chickpeas

Put 60 ml (2 fl oz/¼ cup) olive oil and 1 chopped onion in a large saucepan and cook over medium heat for 7–8 minutes, or until softened. Stir in 1 finely chopped garlic clove, 1 teaspoon harissa, or to taste (or ¼ teaspoon cayenne pepper), ½ teaspoon paprika, ¼ teaspoon ground ginger, ½ teaspoon ground turmeric, 1 teaspoon ground cumin and 1 teaspoon ground cinnamon and cook gently for 2 minutes. Add 400 g (14 oz) can chopped tomatoes and 1 teaspoon sugar and season, to taste. Cover and simmer for 20 minutes. Meanwhile, drain 2 x 425 g (15 oz) cans chickpeas and put them in a large bowl with enough cold water to cover well. Lift up handfuls of chickpeas and rub them between your hands to loosen the skins. Run more water into the bowl, stir well and let the skins float to the top, then skim them off. Repeat until all the skins have been removed. Drain the chickpeas again and stir them into the tomato mixture. Cover and simmer for 20–25 minutes, adding a little more water if necessary. Stir through 3 tablespoons chopped flat-leaf (Italian) parsley and 2 tablespoons chopped coriander (cilantro) leaves and season, to taste. Serve with crusty bread or with couscous. Serves 4.

chickpea and saffron soup

Put 2 tablespoons olive oil and 1 finely chopped onion in a large saucepan. Cook over low heat for 5 minutes to soften. Add 1 crushed garlic clove and ¼ teaspoon each of ground ginger, turmeric and pepper and cook for a few seconds. Stir in 1 litre (35 fl oz/4 cups) chicken or vegetable stock, ¼ teaspoon ground saffron threads, 1 tablespoon tomato paste (purée) and 3 tablespoons chopped flat-leaf (Italian) parsley. Drain and rinse a 425 g (15 oz) can chickpeas and add to the pan. Bring to the boil, cover and simmer gently for 40 minutes. Season, to taste, and serve hot. Serves 4.

spiced lentil and pumpkin tagine

serves 4–6

THERE ARE FEW TRULY VEGETARIAN RECIPES IN MOROCCAN COOKING, BUT THIS IS ONE OF THEM, AND A DELICIOUS AND NUTRITIOUS ONE AT THAT. THE EARTHY FLAVOUR OF LENTILS COMBINES WITH THE SWEETNESS OF THE PUMPKIN, THE FLAVOURS MELDING WITH TRADITIONAL HERBS AND SPICES.

brown lentils	275 g (9¾ oz/1½ cups)
tomatoes	2
firm pumpkin or butternut pumpkin (squash)	600 g (1 lb 5 oz)
olive oil	60 ml (2 fl oz/¼ cup)
onion	1, finely chopped
garlic	3 cloves, finely chopped
ground cumin	½ teaspoon
ground turmeric	½ teaspoon
cayenne pepper	⅛ teaspoon (or 1 teaspoon harissa, or to taste)
paprika	1 teaspoon
tomato paste (purée)	3 teaspoons
sugar	½ teaspoon
flat-leaf (Italian) parsley	1 tablespoon finely chopped
coriander (cilantro)	2 tablespoons chopped leaves

Rinse the lentils in a sieve. Tip into a saucepan and add 1 litre (35 fl oz/4 cups) cold water. Bring to the boil, skim the surface if necessary, then cover and simmer over low heat for 20 minutes.

Meanwhile, halve the tomatoes horizontally and squeeze out the seeds. Coarsely grate the tomatoes into a bowl down to the skin, discarding the skin. Set the tomato aside. Peel and seed the pumpkin and cut into 3 cm (1¼ in) dice. Set aside.

Heat the oil in a large saucepan, add the onion and cook over low heat until softened. Add the garlic, cook for a few seconds, then stir in the cumin, turmeric and cayenne pepper or harissa. Cook for 30 seconds, then add the grated tomatoes, paprika, tomato paste, sugar, half the parsley and coriander, 1 teaspoon salt and freshly ground black pepper, to taste. Add the drained lentils and chopped pumpkin, stir well, then cover and simmer for 20 minutes, or until the pumpkin and lentils are tender. Adjust the seasoning and sprinkle with the remaining parsley and coriander. Serve hot or warm with crusty bread.

There is considerable confusion in some quarters as to what constitutes a pumpkin. The large, orange pumpkin with fibrous flesh is often looked upon with disdain, but can be good for soups and purées. If only these are available, choose small specimens. However, the pumpkins also known as winter squash are an entirely different matter. Choose those that have a firm orange flesh and are of a reasonable size. Butternut pumpkin (squash) is a variety that is more widely available, but experiment with what is available in your area.

chicken k'dra with chickpeas . . . . serves 4

A K'DRA IS A BERBER METHOD OF COOKING CHICKEN, CHARACTERIZED BY THE LARGE AMOUNT OF HERBED SMEN AND ONIONS USED, AS WELL AS CHICKPEAS AND SAFFRON. THE AMOUNT OF SMEN (CLARIFIED BUTTER) IN THE FOLLOWING RECIPE HAS BEEN REDUCED. BUTTER CAN BE USED INSTEAD OF THE SMEN.

smen or butter	60 g (2¼ oz)
onions	3, thinly sliced
ground ginger	½ teaspoon
freshly ground black pepper	½ teaspoon
chicken	1.5 kg (3 lb 5 oz), quartered
ground saffron threads	¼ teaspoon
cinnamon stick	1
chickpeas	2 x 425 g (15 oz) cans
flat-leaf (Italian) parsley	3 tablespoons finely chopped, plus extra, to serve
lemon wedges	to serve

Melt the smen or butter in a large saucepan. Add a third of the onion and cook over medium heat for 5 minutes, or until softened. Add the ginger, pepper and chicken pieces and cook without browning for 2–3 minutes, turning the chicken occasionally. Add the remaining onion, about 300 ml (10½ fl oz) water, the saffron, cinnamon stick and 1 teaspoon salt. Bring to a slow boil, reduce the heat to low, then cover and simmer gently for 45 minutes.

Meanwhile, drain the chickpeas and place them in a large bowl with cold water to cover. Lift up handfuls of chickpeas and rub them between your hands to loosen the skins, dropping them back into the bowl. Run more water into the bowl, stir well and let the skins float to the top, then skim them off. Repeat until all the skins have been removed. Add the skinned chickpeas to the chicken, along with the chopped parsley, stir gently, then cover and simmer for 15 minutes, or until the chicken is tender.

Tilt the saucepan, spoon off some of the fat from the surface and put it into a frying pan. Lift out the chicken pieces, allowing the sauce to drain back into the saucepan. Heat the fat in the frying pan and brown the chicken pieces quickly over high heat. Meanwhile, boil the sauce to reduce it a little.

Serve the chicken with the chickpeas and the sauce spooned over. Sprinkle with the extra parsley and serve with lemon wedges and crusty bread.

Cover the drained chickpeas with cold water.

Skim off the chickpea skins as they float to the top.

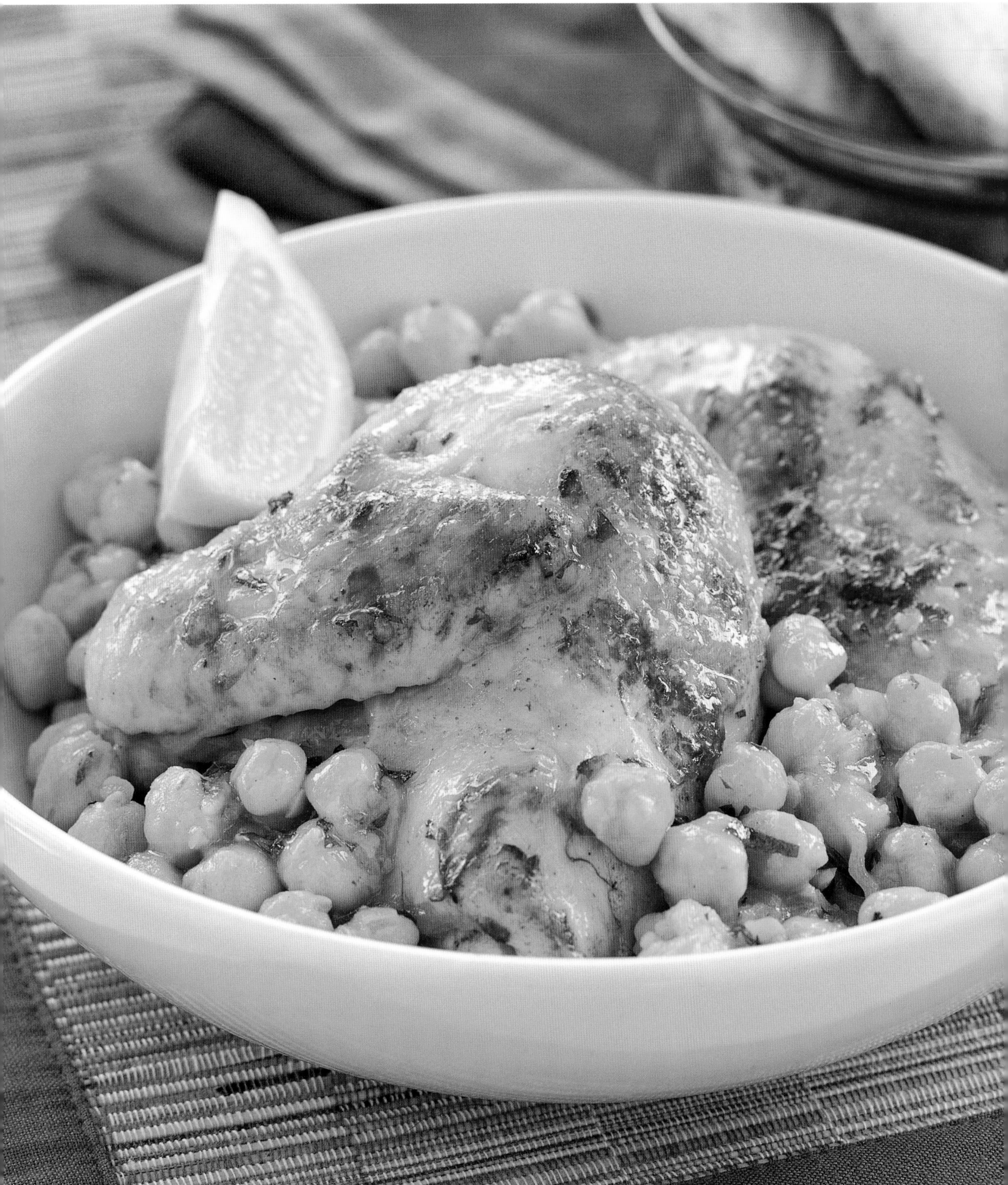

lamb tagine with
sweet tomato jam .... serves 4–6

TOMATO JAM IS SERVED AS AN APPETIZER, LIKE A DIP, BUT THE SAME INGREDIENTS COMBINE WITH LAMB TO GIVE A BEAUTIFULLY FLAVOURED TAGINE, REDOLENT WITH CINNAMON AND HONEY. IT IS PREFERABLE TO USE FRESH TOMATOES RATHER THAN CANNED.

olive oil	2 tablespoons
lamb shoulder or leg steaks	1 kg (2 lb 4 oz), trimmed and cut into 3 cm (1 1/4 in) thick pieces
onions	2, coarsely grated
ripe tomatoes	1.5 kg (3 lb 5 oz), halved horizontally
garlic	2 cloves, finely chopped
ground ginger	1 teaspoon
freshly ground black pepper	1/4 teaspoon
cinnamon stick	1
tomato paste (purée)	60 g (2 1/4 oz / 1/4 cup)
ground saffron threads	1/8 teaspoon, optional
butter	30 g (1 oz)
blanched almonds	40 g (1 1/2 oz / 1/4 cup)
honey	2 tablespoons
ground cinnamon	1 1/2 teaspoons

Heat half the oil in a heavy-based saucepan over high heat and brown the lamb, in batches. Remove and set aside. Reduce the heat to low, add the remaining oil and the onion and cook gently, stirring occasionally, for 10 minutes, or until the onion is softened.

Meanwhile, squeeze out the tomato seeds. Coarsely grate the tomatoes down to the skin, discarding the skin. Stir the garlic, ginger, pepper and cinnamon into the pan and cook for 1 minute. Add the tomato paste and saffron, if using, and cook for 1 minute. Return the lamb to the pan, stir in the grated tomato and season. Cover and simmer gently for 1 1/4 hours. Simmer, partly covered, for 15 minutes, stirring occasionally, then simmer, uncovered, for 25 minutes, or until the sauce has thickened and has an almost jam-like consistency with the oil beginning to separate.

Meanwhile, melt the butter in a small frying pan, add the almonds and cook over medium heat, stirring occasionally, until golden. Stir the honey and ground cinnamon into the tagine and simmer for 2 minutes. Serve with couscous, sprinkled with the almonds.

The finely shaved bark of the cinnamon tree, *Cinnamomum zeylanicum*, is interleaved and rolled to form sticks or quills about 8 cm (3 1/4 in) long. Cassia is from another species of cinnamon tree, *Cinnamomum cassia*. It has a highly perfumed aroma and is bittersweet. It is also available in sticks made of shaved bark, with 'leaves' visibly thicker than those in cinnamon sticks. It is more reddish-brown than cinnamon but can be used in place of cinnamon sticks; in fact it is often sold as such. Ground cinnamon often includes cassia (if it is brownish-red, it probably contains cassia). Both these spices, ground and in sticks, are used in savoury and sweet dishes and pastries.

three ways with prunes

THE PRUNE IS THE DRIED VERSION OF VARIOUS SPECIES OF THE DAMASCENE (DAMSON) PLUM. IT IS OFTEN A SUBSTITUTE FOR DATES IN MEAT AND FRUIT TAGINES, BUT IS INCREASINGLY USED IN ITS OWN RIGHT — AN INTENSELY FLAVOURED SWEET–SOUR FRUIT THAT MARRIES WELL WITH SPICES. TODAY'S PRUNES DO NOT NEED SOAKING — THEY ARE MOIST AND SUCCULENT AND ADD A WONDERFUL FLAVOUR TO MOROCCAN DISHES. WHILE IT IS AN EASY (THOUGH SOMEWHAT STICKY) TASK TO REMOVE THE PITS, PITTED PRUNES ARE READILY AVAILABLE.

lamb shank and prune tagine

You will need 4 frenched lamb shanks. (Frenched lamb shanks are trimmed of excess fat with the knuckle end of the bone sawn off.) If unavailable, use whole shanks and ask the butcher to saw them in half for you. Place a heavy-based saucepan over high heat, add 1 tablespoon oil and 30 g (1 oz) butter, then add the lamb shanks. Brown the shanks on all sides and remove to a plate. Reduce the heat to medium, add 1 chopped onion and cook gently for 5 minutes to soften. Add 375 ml (13 fl oz/1 1/2 cups) water, 1/4 teaspoon ground saffron threads, 1/2 teaspoon ground ginger, 2 cinnamon sticks and 4 coriander (cilantro) sprigs, tied in a bunch. Season, to taste. Stir well and return the lamb shanks to the pan. Cover and simmer over low heat for 1 hour. Remove the zest of 1/2 lemon in wide strips. Add to the pan and cook for a further 30 minutes. Add 300 g (10 1/2 oz/1 1/3 cups) pitted prunes and 2 tablespoons honey, cover and simmer for a further 30 minutes until the lamb is very tender. Remove and discard the coriander sprigs. Serve hot, sprinkled with 1 tablespoon roasted sesame seeds. Serves 4.

spiced chicken with prunes

Melt 30 g (1 oz) butter in a lidded frying pan. Add 1 1/2 teaspoons ras el hanout and stir over low heat for 30 seconds. Increase the heat to medium, add 4 x 175 g (6 oz) chicken breast fillets and cook for 1 minute on each side, without allowing the spices to burn. Remove the chicken from the pan. Add 1 sliced onion to the pan and cook over medium heat for 5 minutes. Pour in 250 ml (9 fl oz/ 1 cup) chicken stock and add 150 g (5 1/2 oz/2/3 cup) pitted prunes and 3 teaspoons each of honey, lemon juice and rosewater. Cover and simmer over low heat for 10 minutes. Return the chicken to the pan, cover and simmer gently for 15 minutes. Slice the chicken breasts on the diagonal and serve with the prune sauce and steamed couscous (page 140). Serves 4.

roast vegetables with prunes

Pour 60 ml (2 fl oz/1/4 cup) olive oil into a 30 x 40 x 6 cm (12 x 16 x 2 1/2 in) ovenproof dish and add 2 peeled and quartered red onions, 3 bruised unpeeled garlic cloves and 2 sliced carrots. Toss well. Bake in a preheated 200°C (400°F/Gas 6) oven for 15 minutes. Peel and cut 450 g (1 lb) each of firm pumpkin and orange sweet potato into large cubes. Add to the dish, along with 1 1/2 teaspoons ras el hanout and 1 seeded and sliced red chilli. Season and toss well. Bake for a further 30 minutes. Stir in 375 ml (13 fl oz/1 1/2 cups) light chicken or vegetable stock, 200 g (7 oz/scant 1 cup) pitted prunes and 1 tablespoon honey and return to the oven for a further 30 minutes. Serve with steamed couscous (page 140) or as a vegetable accompaniment. Serves 4.

lamb shank and prune tagine

beef tagine with
sweet potatoes .... serves 4–6

USE THE ORANGE-FLESHED SWEET POTATO AS IT IS MEALY AND SWEET, AND KEEPS ITS SHAPE WHEN COOKED. THE TAGINE IS FINISHED AND BROWNED IN THE OVEN; IN TRADITIONAL MOROCCAN COOKING, IT WOULD BE COVERED WITH A METAL LID WITH GLOWING CHARCOAL PLACED ON TOP — VERY EFFECTIVE.

blade or chuck steak	1 kg (2 lb 4 oz)
olive oil	60 ml (2 fl oz/¼ cup)
onion	1, finely chopped
cayenne pepper	½ teaspoon
ground cumin	½ teaspoon
ground turmeric	1 teaspoon
ground ginger	½ teaspoon
paprika	2 teaspoons
flat-leaf (Italian) parsley	2 tablespoons chopped
coriander (cilantro)	2 tablespoons chopped leaves
tomatoes	2
orange sweet potatoes	500 g (1 lb 2 oz)

Trim the steak of any fat and cut into 2.5 cm (1 in) pieces. Heat half the oil in a saucepan and brown the beef in batches over high heat, adding a little more oil as needed. Set aside in a dish.

Reduce the heat to low, add the onion and the remaining oil to the pan and gently cook for 10 minutes, or until the onion is softened. Add the cayenne pepper, cumin, turmeric, ginger and paprika, cook for a few seconds, then add 1 teaspoon salt and a good grinding of black pepper. Return the beef to the pan, add the parsley, coriander and 250 ml (9 fl oz/1 cup) water. Cover and simmer over low heat for 1½ hours, or until the meat is almost tender.

Peel the tomatoes. To do this, score a cross in the base of each one using a knife. Put the tomatoes in a bowl of boiling water for 20 seconds, then plunge them into a bowl of cold water to cool. Remove from the water and peel the skin away from the cross — it should slip off easily. Slice the tomatoes. Peel the sweet potatoes, cut them into 2 cm (¾ in) dice and leave in cold water until required, as this will prevent them from discolouring. Preheat the oven to 180°C (350°F/Gas 4).

Transfer the meat and its sauce to an ovenproof serving dish (the base of a tagine would be ideal). Drain the sweet potato and spread it on top of the beef. Top with the tomato slices. Cover with foil (or the lid of the tagine) and bake for 40 minutes. Remove the foil, increase the oven temperature to 220°C (425°F/Gas 7) and raise the dish to the upper oven shelf. Cook until the tomato and sweet potato are flecked with brown and are tender. Serve from the dish.

Peel the skin from the tomatoes before slicing them.

Peel the sweet potatoes and cut them into dice.

lamb tagine with peas and lemons

PRESERVED LEMONS ADD A WONDERFUL FLAVOUR TO THIS DELICIOUS COMBINATION OF LAMB, GREEN PEAS, FRESH HERBS AND GROUND SPICES. WHILE SHELLED FRESH GREEN PEAS ARE PREFERRED, FROZEN PEAS ALSO GIVE GOOD RESULTS.

lamb shoulder or leg	1 kg (2 lb 4 oz), boned
olive oil	2 tablespoons
onion	1, finely chopped
garlic	2 cloves, finely chopped
ground cumin	1 teaspoon
ground ginger	1/2 teaspoon
ground turmeric	1/2 teaspoon
coriander (cilantro)	3 tablespoons chopped leaves
flat-leaf (Italian) parsley	3 tablespoons chopped
lemon thyme	2 teaspoons chopped
preserved lemons	1 1/2
peas	235 g (8 1/2 oz/1 1/2 cups)
chopped mint	2 teaspoons
sugar	1/2 teaspoon

Trim the lamb and cut into 3 cm (1 1/4 in) pieces. Heat the oil in a large saucepan over high heat and brown the lamb, in batches, removing to a dish when cooked. Add more oil if required.

Reduce the heat to low, add the onion and cook for 5 minutes, or until softened. Add the garlic, cumin, ginger and turmeric and cook for a few seconds. Add 375 ml (13 fl oz/1 1/2 cups) water and stir well to lift the browned juices off the base of the pan, then return the lamb to the pan with a little salt and a good grinding of black pepper. Add the coriander, parsley and thyme, cover and simmer over low heat for 1 1/2 hours, or until the lamb is tender.

Separate the preserved lemons into quarters and rinse well under cold running water, removing and discarding the pulp. Cut the rind into strips and add to the lamb, along with the peas, mint and sugar. Return to a simmer, cover and simmer for a further 10 minutes, or until the peas are cooked. Serve hot.

Essential in Moroccan cooking, fresh coriander, also known as cilantro, has feathery green leaves with a somewhat pungent, lemony flavour. It is native to the Middle East and southern Europe, and has been used as a culinary herb for millennia. The plant could have been introduced into the region that is now Morocco from antiquity, as it was favoured by the Greeks and Romans. The dried seeds are ground and used as a spice, with a combined lemon zest and sage flavour. Dried coriander complements cumin but is not used as frequently as cumin; however, it is one of the spices used in ras el hanout (page 113).

kefta tagine . . . . serves 4

FOR COMMUNAL EATING IN THE MOROCCAN MANNER, THIS DISH IS SERVED DIRECTLY AT THE TABLE IN THE DISH IN WHICH IT IS COOKED. WITH THE AID OF BREAD, DINERS MANAGE TO GET THEIR FAIR PORTION OF THE EGG. BREAD IS ALSO A MUST FOR MOPPING UP THE FULL-FLAVOURED SAUCE.

minced (ground) lamb	700 g (1 lb 9 oz)
onion	1 small, finely chopped
garlic	2 cloves, finely chopped
flat-leaf (Italian) parsley	2 tablespoons finely chopped
coriander (cilantro)	2 tablespoons finely chopped leaves
cayenne pepper	1/2 teaspoon
ground ginger	1/2 teaspoon
ground cumin	1 teaspoon
paprika	1 teaspoon
oil	2 tablespoons

sauce

olive oil	2 tablespoons
onion	1, finely chopped
garlic	2 cloves, finely chopped
ground cumin	2 teaspoons
ground cinnamon	1/2 teaspoon
paprika	1 teaspoon
chopped tomatoes	800 g (1 lb 12 oz) can
harissa	2 teaspoons, or to taste
coriander (cilantro)	4 tablespoons chopped leaves
eggs	4

Put the lamb, onion, garlic, herbs and spices in a bowl and mix well. Season with salt and freshly ground black pepper. Roll tablespoons of the mixture into balls.

Heat the oil in a large lidded frying pan over medium to high heat, add the meatballs in batches and cook, turning occasionally, for 8–10 minutes, or until browned all over. Remove the meatballs and set aside in a bowl. Wipe the frying pan with paper towels.

To make the sauce, heat the olive oil in the frying pan, add the onion and cook over medium heat for 5 minutes, or until the onion is soft. Add the garlic, cumin, cinnamon and paprika and cook for 1 minute, or until fragrant. Stir in the tomato and harissa and bring to the boil. Reduce the heat and simmer for 20 minutes.

Add the meatballs, cover and simmer for 10 minutes, or until cooked. Stir in the coriander, then carefully break the eggs into the simmering tagine and cook until just set. (Alternatively, transfer the meatballs and sauce to a large shallow ovenproof serving dish. Add the eggs and cook in a preheated 200°C (400°F/Gas 6) oven for 5–8 minutes, or until the eggs are set.) Season and serve with crusty bread to mop up the juices.

Roll tablespoons of the lamb mixture into balls.

Carefully break 4 eggs into the simmering tagine.

three ways with pumpkin

THE MOROCCAN PUMPKIN, KAR'A LHAMRA, IS ROUND AND ORANGE-SKINNED, AND FIRMER AND SWEETER THAN THE JACK'O'LANTERN-TYPE. THE BUTTERNUT PUMPKIN (SQUASH) IS ALSO USED; OTHER WINTER SQUASH IS SUITABLE SO LONG AS IT IS HEAVY FOR ITS SIZE, THE FLESH IS FIRM, SWEET AND ORANGE-COLOURED, AND IT HAS A HARD SKIN THAT HAS TO BE PEELED. PUMPKIN IS USED FOR VEGETABLE TAGINES, AS A WARM SALAD OR APPETIZER THAT CAN ACCOMPANY MAIN MEALS, AND OFTEN IN STEWS FOR SERVING WITH COUSCOUS.

pumpkin and sweet potato tagine

Peel and cube 600 g (1 lb 5 oz) butternut pumpkin (squash) or other firm pumpkin and 500 g (1 lb 2 oz) orange sweet potato. Melt 60 g (2¼ oz) butter in a large saucepan over low heat. Add 1 finely chopped large onion and cook gently, stirring occasionally, until softened. Add 2 finely chopped garlic cloves, 1 teaspoon each of ground ginger and turmeric, 1 cinnamon stick and a pinch of cayenne pepper. Stir over low heat for 1–2 minutes. Pour in 500 ml (17 fl oz/2 cups) vegetable or chicken stock, add ⅛ teaspoon ground saffron threads, then increase the heat to medium and bring to the boil. Add the pumpkin, sweet potato, 60 g (2¼ oz/½ cup) raisins and 1 tablespoon honey and season with salt and freshly ground black pepper. Cover and simmer for a further 15 minutes, or until the vegetables are tender. Remove the cinnamon stick, transfer the tagine to a bowl and scatter with coriander (cilantro) leaves. Serve with couscous or as an accompaniment. Serves 4–6.

warm pumpkin salad with preserved lemon

Peel and remove the seeds from 1 kg (2 lb 4 oz) firm pumpkin or butternut pumpkin (squash). Cut the pumpkin into 2 cm (¾ in) cubes. Remove the pulp from 1 preserved lemon and rinse and dice the rind. Heat 60 ml (2 fl oz/¼ cup) olive oil in a large lidded frying pan. Add 1 grated onion and cook over medium heat for 3 minutes. Stir in ½ teaspoon each of ground ginger and cumin and 1 teaspoon paprika and cook for a further 30 seconds. Add the pumpkin, 2 tablespoons each of chopped flat-leaf (Italian) parsley and coriander (cilantro) leaves, 1 tablespoon lemon juice, the preserved lemon rind and 125 ml (4 fl oz/½ cup) water. Season, to taste, cover and simmer over low heat for 20 minutes, or until tender, tossing occasionally with a spatula and adding a little more water if necessary. Serve warm as an appetizer or hot as a vegetable accompaniment. Serves 4.

roast pumpkin with orange and spices

Peel and remove the seeds from 1 kg (2 lb 4 oz) firm pumpkin or butternut pumpkin (squash). Cut the pumpkin into 2 cm (¾ in) cubes. Put the pumpkin in a roasting tin with 2 tablespoons oil and toss to coat. Combine the grated zest and juice of 1 orange and pour over the pumpkin. Sprinkle with 1½ teaspoons ras el hanout, season and drizzle with 3 teaspoons honey. Roast in a preheated 200°C (400°F/Gas 6) oven for 45 minutes, tossing occasionally with a spatula. Serve hot or warm as an appetizer or vegetable accompaniment. Serves 4.

pumpkin and sweet potato tagine

meatball tagine with herbs and lemon

THE MEATBALLS IN THIS DISH DO NOT NEED TO BE BROWNED. SPICES, COMBINED WITH FRESH FLAT-LEAF (ITALIAN) PARSLEY AND CORIANDER (CILANTRO) AND THE HEAT OF FRESH CHILLI, ARE USED WITH LEMON TO MAKE A DELICIOUS SAUCE IN WHICH TO COOK THEM.

onion	1/2, roughly chopped
flat-leaf (Italian) parsley	2 tablespoons roughly chopped
white bread	2 slices, crusts removed
egg	1
minced (ground) lamb or beef	500 g (1 lb 2 oz)
ground cumin	1/2 teaspoon
paprika	1/2 teaspoon
freshly ground black pepper	1/2 teaspoon

herb and lemon sauce

butter or oil	1 tablespoon
onion	1/2, finely chopped
paprika	1/2 teaspoon
ground turmeric	1/2 teaspoon
ground cumin	1/4 teaspoon
red chilli	1, seeded and sliced (or 1/4 teaspoon cayenne pepper)
chicken stock	375 ml (13 fl oz/1 1/2 cups)
coriander (cilantro)	2 tablespoons chopped leaves
flat-leaf (Italian) parsley	2 tablespoons chopped
lemon juice	2 tablespoons
preserved lemon	1/2, optional

Put the onion and parsley in a food processor and process until finely chopped. Tear the bread into pieces, add to the onion, along with the egg and process briefly. Add the lamb or beef, cumin, paprika, pepper and 1 teaspoon salt and process to a thick paste, scraping down the side of the bowl occasionally. Alternatively, grate the onion, chop the parsley, crumb the bread and add to the lamb or beef in a bowl with the egg, spices and seasoning. Knead until paste-like in consistency.

With moistened hands, shape the mixture into walnut-sized balls and place them on a tray. Cover and refrigerate until required.

To make the herb and lemon sauce, heat the butter or oil in a saucepan and add the onion. Cook over low heat until softened and golden, then add the paprika, turmeric, cumin and chilli or cayenne pepper and cook, stirring, for 1 minute. Add the chicken stock and coriander and bring to the boil.

Add the meatballs to the pan, shaking so that they settle into the sauce. Cover and simmer for 45 minutes. Add most of the parsley and the lemon juice and season if necessary. Return to the boil and simmer for 2 minutes. If using preserved lemon, rinse well under running water, remove and discard the pulp and cut the rind into strips. Add to the meatballs. Transfer to a tagine or bowl, scatter with the remaining parsley and serve hot with crusty bread.

vegetables with lamb stuffing

.... serves 4

HERE IS ONE VERSION OF MOROCCAN STUFFED VEGETABLES. MOROCCAN COOKS TAKE THE TIME TO HOLLOW OUT THE ZUCCHINI (COURGETTES) BEFORE FILLING THEM, BUT IT IS ACCEPTABLE TO HALVE THEM, SCOOP OUT THE CENTRES, FILL THEM WITH THE STUFFING AND REASSEMBLE.

zucchini (courgettes)	4 medium
capsicums (peppers)	2 small
tomatoes	6
olive oil	2 tablespoons
onion	1, finely chopped
garlic	2 cloves, finely chopped
ground ginger	1/2 teaspoon
ground cinnamon	1/2 teaspoon
freshly ground black pepper	1/4 teaspoon
minced (ground) lamb or beef	500 g (1 lb 2 oz)
flat-leaf (Italian) parsley	2 tablespoons chopped
coriander (cilantro)	1 tablespoon chopped leaves
mint	2 teaspoons chopped
short-grain rice	55 g (2 oz/1/4 cup)

tomato sauce

tomato	1 large
olive oil	1 tablespoon
onion	1, coarsely grated
garlic	1 clove, finely chopped
paprika	1/2 teaspoon
ground cumin	1/4 teaspoon
tomato paste (purée)	2 tablespoons
sugar	1 teaspoon
lemon juice	1 tablespoon

Halve the zucchini lengthways. Scoop out the centres, leaving a 1 cm (1/2 in) border. Halve the capsicums lengthways; remove the seeds and membrane. Slice the tops from 4 tomatoes (reserve the tops), scoop out the centres and rub the pulp through a sieve into a bowl and set aside. Peel the remaining tomatoes by scoring a cross in the base of each one using a knife. Put them in a bowl of boiling water for 20 seconds, then plunge them into a bowl of cold water to cool. Remove from the water and peel the skin away from the cross — it should slip off easily. Thinly slice the tomatoes and set aside.

Put the oil and onion in a pan and cook over medium heat for 5 minutes. Stir in the garlic, ginger, cinnamon and pepper, then stir in the lamb or beef. Add 250 ml (9 fl oz/1 cup) water, the parsley, coriander, mint and 1 teaspoon salt. Bring to the boil, then cover and simmer over low heat for 20 minutes. Stir in the rice, cover and cook for 10 minutes, or until most of the liquid has been absorbed.

To make the tomato sauce, first peel the tomato (see above). Halve the tomato horizontally and squeeze out the seeds. Chop the tomato and add to the reserved tomato pulp, along with the remaining sauce ingredients and 125 ml (4 fl oz/1/2 cup) water. Season, to taste. Preheat the oven to 180°C (350°F/Gas 4).

Loosely fill the vegetables with the stuffing. Fill four zucchini halves and top each with an unfilled half, securing with wooden cocktail picks. Fill the capsicums and arrange tomato slices over the top; fill the tomatoes and replace the tops. Arrange the vegetables in an ovenproof dish. Pour in the sauce, cover with foil and bake for 50 minutes, then remove the foil, baste the vegetables with sauce and cook for 10 minutes, or until tender. Remove the picks from the zucchini and serve.

Scoop out the centres of the zucchini, leaving a border.

Loosely fill the vegetables with the stuffing.

fish tagine with tomato and potato

WHEN COOKING FISH IN A TAGINE, MOROCCAN COOKS PREVENT IT FROM STICKING TO THE BASE OF THE TAGINE BY USING CRISSCROSSED BAMBOO CANES, PIECES OF CELERY OR STICKS OF CARROT. THE POTATO SLICES USED IN THIS RECIPE SERVE THE SAME PURPOSE, AND BECOME A DELICIOUS PART OF THE DISH.

chermoula

garlic	2 cloves, roughly chopped
flat-leaf (Italian) parsley	3 tablespoons chopped
coriander (cilantro)	3 tablespoons chopped leaves
paprika	2 teaspoons
ground cumin	2 teaspoons
cayenne pepper	1/4 teaspoon
lemon juice	1 tablespoon
olive oil	2 tablespoons
firm white fish cutlets (steaks), such as snapper, blue eye cod, hake or sea bass	4 x 2 cm (3/4 in) thick
potatoes	500 g (1 lb 2 oz)
tomatoes	375 g (13 oz)
green capsicum (pepper)	1
tomato paste (purée)	1 1/2 tablespoons
sugar	1 teaspoon
lemon juice	1 tablespoon
olive oil	2 tablespoons
flat-leaf (Italian) parsley	1 tablespoon chopped
coriander (cilantro)	1 tablespoon chopped

To make the chermoula, use a mortar and pestle to pound the garlic to a paste with 1/2 teaspoon salt. Add the parsley, coriander, paprika, cumin, cayenne pepper and lemon juice. Pound the mixture to a rough paste and then work in the olive oil.

Rub half the chermoula on each side of the fish, place the fish in a dish, then cover and set aside for 20 minutes.

Cut the potatoes and tomatoes into 5 mm (1/4 in) thick slices. Remove the seeds and white membrane from the capsicum and cut into strips of the same thickness. Preheat the oven to 200°C (400°F/Gas 6).

Brush a 30 x 40 x 6 cm (12 x 16 x 2 1/2 in) ovenproof dish with oil. Place a layer of potato slices in the bottom. Put the fish on top. Toss the remaining potato slices with the remaining chermoula and arrange over the fish. Top the tagine with the tomato slices and capsicum strips. Mix the tomato paste with 125 ml (4 fl oz/ 1/2 cup) water and add 1/2 teaspoon salt, a good grinding of black pepper, the sugar, lemon juice and olive oil. Pour over the fish and sprinkle with the combined parsley and coriander.

Cover the dish with foil and bake for 40 minutes, then remove the foil and move the dish to the upper shelf. Cook for a further 10 minutes, or until the fish and potato are tender and the top is lightly crusted. Serve hot.

Add the herbs, spices and lemon juice to the garlic paste.

Work the olive oil into the chermoula paste.

the souks

The souks, or markets, of Morocco are just one of the places from which Moroccans buy their foods, but these are by far the most fascinating, especially those located within the ancient walls of the medina, the ancient Arab quarter. Rows of small stalls, their tables piled high with the season's produce, provide a riot of magnificent colour — rich red tomatoes, a tumble of bright orange carrots, glossy green and red capsicums (peppers), purple eggplants (aubergines), red, golden and white onions, crisp white turnips, waxy green cucumbers and zucchini (courgettes), red and white radishes and young green peas.

Men sit at their stalls, offering wild artichokes, tender wild asparagus, fragrant strawberries or freshly laid eggs from their woven baskets or wooden crates. Nearby, a trolley might be laden with coriander (cilantro), another with fragrant mint, while the smell of freshly baked bread wafts from a cloth-covered table of wooden crates. Open-fronted shops display an array of spices, as well as a selection of olives and preserved lemons, fresh dates, figs, nuts and raisins, chickpeas and couscous, or slabs of nougat studded with almonds.

The stalls of the meat market are jammed too. Sides of lamb hang from the roof, camel haunches are on offer, and there are cages holding rabbits, chickens, ducks and pigeons. These are usually sold live, but the poultry seller will dispatch and pluck the birds on request.

Shoppers move purposefully, male shoppers bargaining for the best price. The haggling, the shouting, the braying of donkeys, the smell of kebabs cooking, the pervading aromas of spices and mint all combine to make shopping in the souk an unforgettable experience.

tagine of lamb, olives and potatoes

serves 4–6

SAFFRON PERFUMES THE POTATOES AND GIVES THEM A GOLDEN GLOW. IF YOU CAN PURCHASE CRACKED GREEN OLIVES, SO MUCH THE BETTER: BLANCH THEM FOR 2 MINUTES ONLY EACH TIME, AS THE BITTERNESS CAN BE REMOVED MORE READILY.

boneless lamb shoulder	1 kg (2 lb 4 oz)
olive oil	80 ml (2 1/2 fl oz/1/3 cup)
onions	2, finely chopped
garlic	2 cloves, finely chopped
ground cumin	1 teaspoon
ground ginger	1/2 teaspoon
paprika	1/2 teaspoon
coriander (cilantro)	3 tablespoons chopped leaves
flat-leaf (Italian) parsley	3 tablespoons chopped
green olives	175 g (6 oz/1 cup)
potatoes	750 g (1 lb 10 oz) medium
ground saffron threads	1/4 teaspoon

Trim the lamb and cut it into 3 cm (1 1/4 in) thick pieces. Heat 1 1/2 tablespoons of the olive oil in a large saucepan over high heat and brown the lamb on each side, in batches, removing to a dish when done. Add a little more oil as required.

Reduce the heat to low, add another 1 1/2 tablespoons of olive oil and cook the onion for 5 minutes, or until softened. Add the garlic, cumin and ginger and cook for a few seconds. Add 375 ml (13 fl oz/1 1/2 cups) water and stir well to lift the browned juices off the base of the pan. Return the lamb to the pan, along with the paprika, 1/2 teaspoon salt and a good grinding of black pepper. Add the coriander and parsley, then cover and simmer over low heat for 1–1 1/4 hours.

Meanwhile, put the olives in a small saucepan, cover with water, then bring to the boil and cook for 5 minutes. Drain and repeat once more to sweeten the flavour. Add the drained olives to the lamb, cover and cook for a further 15–30 minutes, or until the lamb is tender.

Peel the potatoes and cut them into quarters. Put in a pan, cover with lightly salted water and add the saffron. Bring to the boil and cook for 10 minutes, or until tender. Drain and toss lightly with the remaining olive oil.

Transfer the lamb and sauce to a serving dish, arrange the potatoes around the lamb and serve.

couscous with chicken and vegetables

.... serves 4

THIS IS ONE OF THE MOST FREQUENTLY PREPARED COUSCOUS DISHES IN MOROCCAN HOUSEHOLDS ON FRIDAYS — THE TRADITIONAL DAY FOR SERVING COUSCOUS. PRESENT IT AS DESCRIBED BELOW, OR ARRANGE THE CHICKEN AND VEGETABLES ON A PLATTER, WITH THE COUSCOUS AND SAUCE SERVED SEPARATELY.

tomatoes	3
smen or ghee	3 tablespoons
chicken	1.6 kg (3 lb 8 oz), cut into 8 pieces
onion	1, finely chopped
ground turmeric	1/2 teaspoon
ground cumin	1/2 teaspoon
pearl or pickling (boiling) onions	8, trimmed
ground saffron threads	1/4 teaspoon
cinnamon stick	1
coriander (cilantro)	4 sprigs
flat-leaf (Italian) parsley	4 sprigs
carrots	3, cut into chunks
zucchini (courgettes)	4, cut into chunks
peas	200 g (7 oz/1 1/3 cups)
	(or very young broad (fava) beans)

spiced couscous

couscous	1 quantity (page 140)
smen or butter	3 tablespoons
chickpeas	425 g (15 oz) can, rinsed and drained
harissa	3 teaspoons, or to taste

First peel the tomatoes by scoring a cross in the base of each one using a knife. Put them in a bowl of boiling water for 20 seconds, then plunge them into a bowl of cold water to cool. Remove from the water and peel the skin away from the cross — it should slip off easily. Cut the tomatoes in half horizontally and squeeze out the seeds. Chop the tomatoes and set aside.

Heat the smen or ghee in a large saucepan or the base of a large couscoussier, add the chicken and brown briefly on each side. Reduce the heat, add the onion and cook gently until the onion has softened. Stir in the turmeric and cumin and add the onions. Pour in 750 ml (26 fl oz/3 cups) water, then add the saffron, cinnamon stick and chopped tomatoes. Tie the coriander and parsley sprigs in a bunch and add to the pan. Season with 1 1/2 teaspoons salt and freshly ground black pepper. Bring to a gentle boil, cover and cook over low heat for 25 minutes. Add the carrot to the pan and simmer for a further 20 minutes. Add the zucchini and peas or broad beans and cook for 15–20 minutes, or until the chicken and vegetables are tender.

Meanwhile, to make the spiced couscous, prepare and steam the couscous as directed, either over the stew or over a saucepan of boiling water, or in the microwave oven. Stir the smen or butter through the couscous.

Heat the chickpeas in a saucepan with 60 ml (2 fl oz/1/4 cup) water, tossing frequently, until the water evaporates. Add to the couscous and stir through.

Pile the couscous on a large, warm platter, make a dent in the centre and ladle the chicken and vegetables on top, letting some tumble down the sides. Moisten with some of the broth from the stew. Put about 250 ml (9 fl oz/1 cup) of the broth into a bowl and stir in the harissa. Add the harissa-flavoured broth to the couscous to keep it moist, and according to individual taste.

couscous with lamb and seven vegetables .... serves 4–5

THE NUMBER SEVEN IS CONSIDERED AUSPICIOUS IN MOROCCO, HENCE THE SEVEN VEGETABLES IN THIS DISTINCTIVE DISH. THE TURNIPS SHOULD BE YOUNG AND CRISP — DO NOT USE SWEDE (RUTABAGA) AS A SUBSTITUTE AS THE FLAVOUR IS TOO STRONG.

lamb shoulder	1 kg (2 lb 4 oz), boned
olive oil	60 ml (2 fl oz/1/4 cup)
onions	2, quartered
garlic	2 cloves, finely chopped
ground turmeric	1/2 teaspoon
paprika	1/2 teaspoon
ground saffron threads	1/4 teaspoon
coriander (cilantro)	4 sprigs
flat-leaf (Italian) parsley	4 sprigs
cinnamon stick	1
chopped tomatoes	400 g (14 oz) can
freshly ground black pepper	1 1/2 teaspoons
carrots	3, cut into thick sticks
turnips	3 small, peeled and quartered
firm pumpkin or butternut pumpkin (squash)	400 g (14 oz)
raisins	30 g (1 oz/1/4 cup)
zucchini (courgettes)	4, cut into sticks
chickpeas	425 g (15 oz) can, rinsed and drained
couscous	1 quantity (page 140)
harissa	2–3 teaspoons, to taste

Trim the lamb of excess fat if necessary. Cut the lamb into 2 cm (3/4 in) cubes. Heat the oil in a large saucepan or the base of a large couscoussier and add the lamb, onion and garlic. Cook over medium heat, turning the lamb once, just until the lamb loses its red colour. Stir in the turmeric, paprika and saffron and add 750 ml (26 fl oz/3 cups) water. Tie the coriander and parsley in a bunch and add it to the pan, along with the cinnamon stick and tomatoes. Add the pepper and 1 1/2 teaspoons salt, to taste. Bring to a gentle boil, cover and simmer over low heat for 1 hour. Add the carrot and turnip and cook for a further 20 minutes.

Meanwhile, peel the pumpkin and cut it into 2.5 cm (1 in) chunks. Add the pumpkin to the pan, along with the raisins, zucchini and chickpeas, adding a little water if necessary to almost cover the ingredients. Cook for a further 20 minutes, or until the meat and vegetables are tender.

Meanwhile, prepare and steam the couscous as directed, either over the stew or over a saucepan of boiling water, or in the microwave oven.

Pile the couscous on a deep, heated platter and make a dent in the centre. Remove the herbs and cinnamon stick from the stew and ladle the meat and vegetables on top of the couscous, letting some tumble down the sides. Moisten with a little broth from the stew. Pour about 250 ml (9 fl oz/1 cup) of the remaining broth into a bowl and stir in the harissa. Add the harissa-flavoured broth to the couscous to keep it moist, according to individual taste.

dishes from the palace

It was in the palaces of the ruling Berber dynasties of the fourteenth century that Moroccan cooking began to take shape. The lavish court kitchens were the conduit by which new foods and recipes were eventually introduced to household kitchens. Women were always employed as cooks, and even today, in the palaces of the reigning monarch and in restaurant kitchens, women still do most of the cooking. Today the Royal Cooking School, set up by King Hussein II in his Rabat Palace complex, still continues the tradition of being the training ground for future chefs as well as cooks in their own households.

Originating in the palaces, the Moroccan diffa (banquet) is a showcase of the skills of Moroccan cooks, when the female family members prepare the food. Betrothals, weddings, births and religious festivals are occasions to celebrate with abundance. Especially lavish diffas are given when a Moroccan returns from a pilgrimage to Mecca.

Seated about low, round tables, on divans luxurious with multicoloured cushions, guests feast on many little dishes before the bisteeya is served in all its glory. This famous pigeon (or chicken) pie was created over many years in palace kitchens, and is considered one of the high points of Moroccan cuisine.

Tagines of meat, poultry and fish follow, including one or more that are sweet with fruit and honey. Chicken, preserved lemon and olive tagine, chicken with apricots and honey, lamb with eggs and almonds, lamb with dates, beef with apples and raisins, whole fish stuffed with almond-filled dates and finished with an almond crust… Herbs and spice mixes flavour them, orange flower water or rosewater perfume some of them, roasted almonds or sesame seeds are strewn over them. And to follow these, couscous — at least two versions, one containing lamb that is sweet with fruit and honey. Platters of fresh fruit nestled in ice complete the feast, followed by mint tea served with great ceremony.

From palace cooking to the humble Moroccan kitchen — it took a few hundred years, but the road thus travelled has given the cooking of Morocco a formidable reputation.

briouats with goat's cheese .... makes 24

THESE ARE TRADITIONALLY MADE WITH WARKHA PASTRY, WHICH IS MADE BY DABBING A BALL OF DOUGH ON A HEATED, UPTURNED COPPER PAN UNTIL THE DOUGH BECOMES A FINE, ALMOST TRANSPARENT SHEET. SPRING ROLL AND WON TON WRAPPERS CAN BE SUBSTITUTED FOR FRIED PASTRIES AND FILO FOR BAKED PASTRIES.

cheese filling

fresh goat's cheese	250 g (9 oz)
flat-leaf (Italian) parsley	3 tablespoons finely chopped
mint	2 teaspoons finely chopped
paprika	1/2 teaspoon
freshly ground black pepper	1/4 teaspoon
egg	1, lightly beaten
won ton wrappers	24
egg white	1, lightly beaten
oil	for deep-frying

To make the cheese filling, mix the cheese with the parsley, mint, paprika and black pepper. Check for salt and add if necessary. Stir in the beaten egg gradually, adding just enough to retain a fairly stiff mixture — if too loose the rolls will be difficult to shape.

Put a stack of won ton wrappers in the folds of a tea towel to prevent them drying out, or cover them with plastic wrap. Place a wrapper on the work surface with one corner of the square towards you and brush around the edge with the egg white. Put 2 teaspoons of cheese filling across the corner, just meeting the sides. Roll once, turn each side of the wrapper over the filling and roll to the end. Place seam side down on a cloth-covered tray. Continue in this manner with the remaining ingredients.

Heat the oil to 180°C (350°F), or until a cube of bread dropped into the hot oil browns in 15 seconds. Add four briouats at a time and fry until golden, turning to brown evenly. Remove with a slotted spoon and drain on paper towels. Serve hot.

Brush around the edge of the wrapper with egg white.

Put 2 teaspoons of the filling on each wrapper and roll up.

mezghaldi of onions
with eggplant..serves 4

THESE SPICY, CARAMELIZED ONIONS ARE USUALLY SERVED ON THEIR OWN AS AN APPETIZER SALAD, BUT CAN ALSO BE TEAMED WITH CHARGRILLED EGGPLANT (AUBERGINE). USE THEM AS AN ACCOMPANIMENT TO CHARGRILLED MEATS OR CHICKEN.

onions	4
olive oil	100 ml (3¹/₂ fl oz)
ground saffron threads	¹/₂ teaspoon
ground ginger	1 teaspoon
ground cinnamon	1 teaspoon
ground allspice	¹/₂ teaspoon
honey	1¹/₂ tablespoons
long thin eggplants (augerbines)	600 g (1 lb 5 oz)

Halve the onions lengthways and cut them into slender wedges. Put them in a lidded frying pan, cover with cold water and bring to the boil. Cover and simmer for 5 minutes. Drain the onion in a colander.

Add 2 tablespoons of the olive oil to the pan and, over low heat, stir in the saffron, ginger, cinnamon and allspice. Cook for 1 minute, increase the heat to medium and return the onion to the pan. Add the honey and 375 ml (13 fl oz/1¹/₂ cups) water and season with salt and freshly ground black pepper. Stir well, reduce the heat to low, cover and simmer for 40 minutes, then uncover and simmer for a further 10 minutes, or until most of the liquid has evaporated.

Wash and dry the eggplants. Leaving the green stalks on, halve them lengthways and peel off a strip of skin from the underside of each half. Using the remaining oil, brush all the eggplant halves on each side. Cook the eggplant in a heated chargrill pan or on a barbecue grill for 3–4 minutes each side until it is tender, adjusting the heat so it does not burn.

Arrange the eggplant cut side up on a platter or individual plates and season lightly with salt. Top with the onion and pour over any juices from the pan. Serve hot or warm with crusty bread.

Halve the eggplants lengthways, leaving the green stalks attached.

Peel a strip of skin from the underside of each eggplant half.

Cook the eggplant on a chargrill or barbecue until it is tender.

harira .... serves 4

THIS SOUP IS THE CENTREPIECE OF THE 'BREAK FAST' MEAL OF RAMADAN. THE FLAVOURSOME LAMB-BASED SOUP IS BOOSTED WITH CHICKPEAS OR LENTILS. IT HAS TO SATISFY HUNGER QUICKLY, SO NOODLES ARE SOMETIMES ADDED, OR IT IS THICKENED WITH YEAST OR FLOUR. VENDORS ALSO SELL IT AS STREET FOOD, LADLED INTO BOWLS.

lamb shoulder steaks	500 g (1 lb 2 oz)
olive oil	2 tablespoons
onions	2 small, chopped
garlic	2 large cloves, crushed
ground cumin	1 1/2 teaspoons
paprika	2 teaspoons
bay leaf	1
tomato paste (purée)	2 tablespoons
beef stock	1 litre (35 fl oz/4 cups)
chickpeas	2 x 425 g (15 oz) cans
chopped tomatoes	800 g (1 lb 12 oz) can
coriander (cilantro)	3 tablespoons finely chopped leaves, plus extra, to serve
flat-leaf (Italian) parsley	3 tablespoons finely chopped
flat bread	to serve

Trim the lamb steaks of excess fat and sinew. Cut the lamb into small chunks.

Heat the olive oil in a large heavy-based saucepan or stockpot, add the onion and garlic and cook over low heat for 5 minutes, or until the onion is soft. Add the meat, increase the heat to medium and stir until the meat changes colour.

Add the cumin, paprika and bay leaf to the pan and cook until fragrant. Add the tomato paste and cook for about 2 minutes, stirring constantly. Add the beef stock to the pan, stir well and bring to the boil.

Drain the chickpeas, rinse them and add to the pan, along with the tomatoes and chopped coriander and parsley. Stir, then bring to the boil. Reduce the heat and simmer for 2 hours, or until the meat is tender. Stir occasionally. Season, to taste. Garnish with the extra coriander and serve with bread.

Chickpeas are the most popular pulse in Morocco, originating in the Middle East and probably introduced by the Romans. Soaked, unskinned chickpeas are used in soups, while skinned chickpeas are preferred in tagines and stews so that flavours can be absorbed. Soak chickpeas overnight; the next day, lift up handfuls of chickpeas and rub them between your hands to loosen the skins, then skim the skins off as they float. Cover the chickpeas with fresh water and boil for at least an hour, until tender, or add to a stew or soup at the start of cooking. Canned chickpeas may also be used, with skins removed in the same way. If preferred, leave skins on for all recipes.

the spice shop

The Arabs had been involved in the spice trade for centuries before their armies
marched forth from Arabia to spread the teachings of the Prophet. When they reached
Morocco in the late seventh century, they brought their spices with them and these
have been part of the Moroccan kitchen ever since.

In the spice shops of the souks, the ground spices — reds, yellows and all shades of
brown — are shaped into smooth mounds in baskets, bins or bowls. Whole spices —
buds, bark, quills, nutmegs, cardamom pods and star anise (recently introduced), tears
of gum arabic, dried chillies and fragrant rosebuds — contrast with the elegant piles of
the ground spices. The mingling aromas give a promise of what they can do to uplift
the forthcoming meal. The eight most important spices for Moroccan cooking are
cinnamon, cumin, saffron (sold in small, clear plastic containers to maintain freshness),
paprika, turmeric, black pepper, fefla soudaniya (similar to cayenne pepper) and ginger.
Then there are cloves, allspice, coriander seeds, fenugreek, aniseed and caraway
seeds. As tempting as the aromas might be, Moroccan cooks only purchase spices
in small amounts to ensure freshness, taking their purchases home in twisted paper
packages to be stored in pottery jars in their kitchens.

Each spice shop has its own ras el hanout, which translates as 'shopkeeper's choice' or 'top of the shop'. This mixture may contain as few as 10 or as many as 26 different ground spices, depending on the whim of the shopkeeper. Spices may include pepper, cayenne pepper, lavender, thyme, rosemary, cumin, ginger, allspice, nutmeg, mace, cardamom, cloves, cinnamon, fenugreek and grains of paradise, also known as melegueta pepper. Orris root, cubeb pepper, belladonna, rosebuds, hashish and other ingredients, some not available outside Morocco, might be included, depending, of course, on the shopkeeper.

For a simplified version of ras el hanout, combine ½ teaspoon each of ground cloves and cayenne pepper, 2 teaspoons each of ground allspice, cumin, ginger, turmeric, black pepper and cardamom, 3 teaspoons each of ground coriander and cinnamon and 2 freshly grated nutmegs or 1½ tablespoons ground nutmeg in a bowl. Mix thoroughly and place in a clean, dry jar. Seal and store in a cool, dark place and use as directed in recipes. Where the flavour of dried rose petals is required, rosewater has been included in recipes to replace the traditional dried rosebuds used in some ras el hanout mixtures.

lamb tagine with dates .... serves 6

IN THIS RICH AND LUSCIOUS DISH, THE DRIED DATES ARE PITTED, AND ARE USED TO THICKEN THE SAUCE, WHICH CARRIES THEIR FLAVOUR THROUGH THE DISH. THE WHOLE DATES USED TO COMPLETE THE DISH ARE LEFT UNPITTED, OTHERWISE THEY CAN DISINTEGRATE.

boneless lamb from shoulder or leg	1 kg (2 lb 4 oz)
butter	30 g (1 oz), plus 15 g (1/2 oz), extra
onion	1, finely chopped
ground ginger	1 teaspoon
ground cinnamon	1 teaspoon
freshly ground black pepper	1/2 teaspoon
dried dates	55 g (2 oz/1/3 cup) pitted and chopped
ground saffron threads	a pinch
honey	2 tablespoons
lemon juice	2 tablespoons
unpitted fresh or dessert dates	200 g (7 oz/1 cup)
preserved lemon	1/2
slivered almonds	40 g (1 1/2 oz/1/3 cup)

Trim the lamb and cut it into 2.5 cm (1 in) cubes. In a large heavy-based saucepan, melt the butter over low heat, add the onion and cook gently until softened. Sprinkle in the ground ginger, cinnamon and black pepper and stir for 1 minute. Increase the heat to high, add the lamb and stir until the colour of the meat changes. Reduce the heat, add 375 ml (13 fl oz/1 1/2 cups) water, the chopped dates and saffron and 1 teaspoon salt, or to taste. Reduce the heat to low, cover and simmer for 1 1/2 hours, stirring occasionally to prevent the sauce sticking as the chopped dates cook to a purée.

Stir in the honey and lemon juice and adjust the seasoning. Put the unpitted dates on top, cover and simmer for 10 minutes, or until the dates are plump.

Meanwhile, rinse the preserved lemon under cold running water, remove and discard the pulp. Drain the rind, pat dry with paper towels and cut into strips. Melt the extra butter in a small frying pan, add the almonds and brown lightly, stirring often. Tip immediately onto a plate to prevent overbrowning.

Remove the whole dates from the top of the lamb and set them aside with the almonds. Ladle the meat into a serving dish or tagine and scatter the dates on top, along with the lemon strips and roasted almonds. Serve hot.

Add the lamb to the onion and spices and cook, stirring.

Put the unpitted dates on top of the lamb mixture.

chicken with preserved lemon and olives . . . . serves 4

ONE OF THE CLASSIC DISHES OF MOROCCO, CALLED DJEJ EMSHMEL, THIS COMBINATION OF SUBTLY SPICED CHICKEN, PRESERVED LEMON AND OLIVES IS USUALLY SERVED AT BANQUETS. USE UNPITTED GREEN OLIVES; IF THEY ARE BITTER, BLANCH THEM IN BOILING WATER FOR 5 MINUTES BEFORE ADDING TO THE CHICKEN.

preserved lemon	¼
olive oil	60 ml (2 fl oz/¼ cup)
chicken	1.6 kg (3 lb 8 oz)
onion	1, chopped
garlic	2 cloves, chopped
chicken stock	625 ml (22 fl oz/2½ cups)
ground ginger	½ teaspoon
ground cinnamon	1½ teaspoons
saffron threads	a pinch
unpitted green olives	100 g (3½ oz/½ cup)
bay leaves	2
chicken livers	2
coriander (cilantro)	3 tablespoons chopped leaves

Rinse the preserved lemon under cold running water, remove and discard the pulp. Drain the rind, pat dry with paper towels and cut into strips. Set aside.

Preheat the oven to 180°C (350°F/Gas 4). Heat 2 tablespoons of the olive oil in a large frying pan, add the chicken and brown on all sides. Place in a deep baking dish.

Heat the remaining oil, add the onion and garlic and cook over medium heat for 3–4 minutes, or until the onion is softened. Add the chicken stock, ginger, cinnamon, saffron, olives, bay leaves and preserved lemon strips and then pour the sauce around the chicken in the dish. Bake for 1½ hours, or until cooked through, adding a little more water or stock if the sauce gets too dry. Baste the chicken during cooking.

Remove the chicken from the dish, cover with foil and leave to rest. Pour the contents of the baking dish into a frying pan, add the chicken livers and mash them into the sauce as they cook. Cook for 5–6 minutes, or until the sauce has reduced and thickened. Add the chopped coriander. Cut the chicken into pieces and serve with the sauce.

Remove the bitter pulp from the preserved lemon.

Cut the preserved lemon rind into thin strips.

chicken with apricots and honey

WHOLE CHICKEN OR CHICKEN CUT INTO PORTIONS IS USUAL IN MOROCCO. HOWEVER, CHICKEN BREASTS, OFF THE BONE AND WITH THE SKIN REMOVED, ARE USED IN THIS DISH TO DECREASE THE COOKING TIME. WHEN FRESH APRICOTS ARE NOT IN SEASON, CANNED APRICOTS ARE A GOOD ALTERNATIVE.

chicken breasts	4 x 175 g (6 oz)
butter	40 g (1 1/2 oz)
ground cinnamon	1 teaspoon
ground ginger	1 teaspoon
freshly ground black pepper	1/4 teaspoon
cayenne pepper	1/8 teaspoon
onion	1, sliced
chicken stock	250 ml (9 fl oz/1 cup)
coriander (cilantro)	6 sprigs, tied in a bunch
apricots	500 g (1 lb 2 oz)
	(or 425 g (15 oz) can apricot halves in natural juice)
honey	2 tablespoons
couscous	1 quantity (page 140)
slivered almonds	2 tablespoons, roasted

Trim the chicken breasts of any fat or gristle. Melt the butter in a large lidded frying pan. Add the spices and stir over low heat for about 1 minute. Increase the heat to medium and add the chicken breasts. Turn them in the spiced butter and cook for 1 minute each side, without allowing the spices to burn.

Add the onion to the pan around the chicken and cook for 5 minutes, stirring the onion and turning the chicken occasionally. Add the stock and coriander sprigs and season if necessary. Reduce the heat to low, cover and simmer for 5 minutes, turning the chicken once.

Wash and halve the apricots and remove the stones. Place them cut side down around the chicken and drizzle with the honey. Cover and simmer for 7–8 minutes, turning the apricots after 5 minutes. Remove the chicken to a plate, cover and rest for 2–3 minutes. Slice each breast on the diagonal.

Prepare and steam the couscous as directed, either over a saucepan of boiling water or in the microwave oven. Put the hot couscous on serving plates and top with the sliced chicken. Remove the coriander sprigs from the sauce and spoon the sauce and apricots over the chicken. Scatter with the almonds and serve hot.

Turn the chicken breasts in the spiced butter.

Drizzle the honey over the apricot halves in the pan.

Turn the apricot halves once during cooking.

Rest the chicken breasts, then slice them on the diagonal.

three ways with citrus

MOROCCO'S CLIMATE IS IDEAL FOR CITRUS FRUITS, ESPECIALLY ORANGES AND LEMONS — BOTH ARE REVERED AND RELISHED. ORANGES ARE COMBINED WITH INGREDIENTS SUCH AS DATES, RADISHES, OLIVES OR CARROTS TO CREATE COOLING SALADS, OR ARE SIMPLY SLICED AND SPRINKLED WITH ORANGE FLOWER WATER, SUGAR AND CINNAMON. FRESH LEMONS MAKE A TART BUT APPETITE-STIMULATING SALAD THAT COMPLEMENTS SWEET SALADS AND TAGINES.

lemon, parsley and onion salad

Peel 6 lemons with a sharp knife, making sure that all the pith and fine membranes are removed, to expose the flesh. Cut the lemons into 1 cm (1/2 in) thick slices and remove the seeds. Dice the lemon slices and put them in a bowl. Halve 1 small red onion, then slice it thinly. Chop 2 large handfuls of flat-leaf (Italian) parsley. Add the onion and parsley to the lemons, along with 1 teaspoon salt and 1 teaspoon caster (superfine) sugar. Toss and set aside for 10 minutes. Just before serving, add a light sprinkling of freshly ground black pepper. Serve this salad with fish, or as a refreshing, tart contrast to tagines that contain fruit. Serves 6–8.

orange and radish salad

Wash and dry 3 sweet oranges, then cut off the tops and bases. Cut the peel off using a sharp knife, removing all traces of pith and cutting through the outer membranes to expose the flesh. Holding the oranges over a small bowl to catch the juice, segment them by cutting between the membranes. Remove the seeds from the orange segments, then put the segments in the bowl. Squeeze the remains of the oranges into the bowl. Drain the orange segments, reserving the orange juice, and return the segments to the bowl. Set the juice aside. Wash 12 red radishes and trim the roots. Slice thinly using a mandolin or vegetable slicer. Add to the orange segments. Put 2 tablespoons of the reserved orange juice in a small bowl, add 1 tablespoon lemon juice, 2 teaspoons caster (superfine) sugar, 2 tablespoons olive oil and a pinch of salt. Beat well and pour over the salad. Sprinkle with 1 tablespoon orange flower water, toss lightly, then cover and chill for 15 minutes. Transfer to a serving bowl, sprinkle the top lightly with ground cinnamon and scatter with small mint leaves. Serves 4.

orange and date salad

Wash and dry 6 sweet oranges, then cut off the tops and bases. Cut the peel off using a sharp knife, removing all traces of pith and cutting through the outer membranes to expose the flesh. Holding the oranges over a bowl to catch the juice, segment them by cutting between the membranes. Remove the seeds and put the segments in the bowl. Squeeze the remains of the oranges over the bowl to extract all the juice. Add 2 teaspoons orange flower water and stir gently to combine. Cover with plastic wrap and refrigerate until chilled. Thinly slice 8 pitted dates lengthways. Lightly roast 90 g (31/4 oz/3/4 cup) slivered almonds. Place the orange segments and juice on a large flat dish and scatter the dates and slivered almonds over the top. Sprinkle small mint leaves over the orange segments. Serve chilled. Serves 4–6.

lemon, parsley and onion salad

tagine of beef
with apples and raisins . . . . serves 6

THIS IS A ROBUST BEEF TAGINE THAT IS SERVED WHEN APPLES ARE IN SEASON, THE TARTNESS OF THE FRUIT MELLOWED WITH THE ADDITION OF RAISINS, SPICES AND HONEY. FOR A REALLY AUTHENTIC FLAVOUR, CHOOSE A THICK, THYME-FLAVOURED HONEY IF POSSIBLE.

chuck or blade steak	1 kg (2 lb 4 oz)
oil	2 tablespoons
butter	40 g (1 1/2 oz)
onion	1, sliced
ground saffron threads	1/4 teaspoon
ground ginger	1/2 teaspoon
ground cinnamon	1 teaspoon, plus 1/2 teaspoon, extra
coriander (cilantro)	4 sprigs, tied in a bunch
raisins	125 g (4 1/2 oz/1 cup)
honey	90 g (3 1/4 oz/1/4 cup)
tart apples, such as Granny Smiths	3, halved, cored and cut into thick wedges
sesame seeds	1 tablespoon, roasted

Trim the beef and cut it into 2.5 cm (1 in) cubes. Heat half the oil and half the butter in a heavy-based saucepan over high heat and brown the beef in batches. Remove to a dish when cooked. Add the remaining oil as needed, and set aside the remaining butter.

Reduce the heat to medium, add the onion and cook for 5 minutes to soften. Add the saffron, ginger and cinnamon and cook for 1 minute. Stir in 375 ml (13 fl oz/1 1/2 cups) water, 1 1/2 teaspoons salt and a generous grinding of black pepper. Return the beef to the pan, along with the coriander. Cover and simmer over low heat for 1 1/2 hours. Add the raisins and 1 tablespoon of the honey, cover and simmer for a further 30 minutes, or until the meat is tender.

Heat the remaining butter in a frying pan and cook the apple for 10 minutes, turning often. Drizzle with the remaining honey, dust with the extra cinnamon and cook for 5 minutes, or until glazed and softened. Transfer the meat and sauce to a serving dish, arrange the apple on top and sprinkle with the sesame seeds.

Hillsides covered with wild thyme and blossoming fruit trees, especially citrus, lure bees to perform their intricate work, often capturing the essence of the blossom in the honey produced. Thyme-flavoured honey is thick with a distinctive flavour just right for adding to tagines; orange blossom honey adds its delicate flavour and aroma to sweet pastries. Light, crumpet-like semolina pancakes, spread with butter while hot and drizzled with ambrosial honey, are a much-loved breakfast treat. Take care when heating honey in which to dip sweet pastries as the honey can scorch easily. Adding a little water can help avoid this.

bisteeya . . . . serves 6–8

THIS CLASSIC PIGEON (OR CHICKEN) PIE TRADITIONALLY IS ENCLOSED IN MOROCCAN WARKHA PASTRY, THEN FRIED, DUSTED WITH POWDERED SUGAR AND DECORATED WITH LINES OF CINNAMON IN A DIAMOND PATTERN. HOWEVER, FILO PASTRY CAN BE USED AND DECORATED WITH A FLURRY OF FILO ON TOP.

smen or butter	250 g (9 oz)
chicken	1.5 kg (3 lb 5 oz), quartered (or 3 x 500 g (1 lb 2 oz) squab (pigeon), halved)
red onions	2 large, finely chopped
garlic	3 cloves, crushed
cinnamon stick	1
ground ginger	1 teaspoon
ground cumin	1 1/2 teaspoons
cayenne pepper	1/4 teaspoon
ground turmeric	1/2 teaspoon
chicken stock	500 ml (17 fl oz/2 cups)
saffron threads	a large pinch, soaked in 2 tablespoons warm water
lemon juice	1 tablespoon
flat-leaf (Italian) parsley	2 large handfuls, chopped
coriander (cilantro)	2 large handfuls leaves, chopped
eggs	5, lightly beaten
almonds	100 g (3 1/2 oz/2/3 cup), roasted, finely chopped
icing (confectioners') sugar	30 g (1 oz/1/4 cup), plus extra, to serve
ground cinnamon	1 teaspoon, plus extra, to serve
filo pastry	12 sheets

Preheat the oven to 160°C (315°F/Gas 2–3). Melt 150 g (5 1/2 oz) of the smen or butter in a large flameproof casserole over medium heat and brown the chicken well. Set aside. Add the onion and cook until golden. Stir in the garlic and spices, then stir in the stock and saffron water. Add the chicken and turn to coat. Cover and bake, turning occasionally, for 1 hour, or until cooked. Add a little extra water if needed. Discard the cinnamon stick. Drain the chicken, remove the meat from the bones and cut it into small pieces. Increase the oven to 180°C (350°F/Gas 4).

Add the lemon juice and herbs to the sauce and reduce over high heat for 10 minutes, or until thick. Reduce the heat to very low, gradually stir in the beaten egg, stirring until scrambled, then remove from the heat. Add the chicken meat and season.

Mix the almonds with the sugar and cinnamon. Melt the remaining smen. Brush a 1.5 litre (52 fl oz/6 cup) deep pie or baking dish with smen. Put a filo sheet over the dish so the edges overhang; brush with smen. Repeat with 7 more sheets, brushing with smen, slightly overlapping the sheets to give a pinwheel effect. Fill with the chicken mixture. Fold 4 of the filo flaps back over, brush with smen and sprinkle with the almond mixture. Fold the remaining flaps over and tuck the edges into the dish. Brush 4 filo sheets with smen, cut into 15 cm (6 in) squares and scrunch into 'flowers' to cover the pie. Bake for 1 hour, or until golden. Serve sprinkled with the combined extra sugar and cinnamon.

Overlap the filo in the pie dish, brushing with the smen.

Sprinkle the almond mixture over the filo.

Scrunch the filo sheets into 'flowers' to cover the pie.

mechoui . . . . serves 6

THIS HOME-COOKED VERSION OF MECHOUI IS A GOOD INDICATION OF THE SUCCULENCE OF SLOW-COOKED LAMB. THE BASTING IS IMPORTANT TO KEEP THE MEAT MOIST AND TO COOK IT TO MELT-IN-THE-MOUTH TENDERNESS. IF THE LAMB BROWNS TOO QUICKLY, MOVE IT TO THE CENTRE OF THE OVEN AND TURN IT OCCASIONALLY.

leg of lamb	2.25 kg (5 lb)
butter	70 g (2½ oz), softened at room temperature
garlic	3 cloves, crushed
ground coriander	3 teaspoons
paprika	1 teaspoon
ground cumin	1½ tablespoons
coarse salt	1½ teaspoons

Preheat the oven to 220°C (425°F/Gas 7). With a small sharp knife, cut small deep slits in the top and sides of the lamb.

Mix the butter, garlic, coriander, paprika, 2 teaspoons of the cumin and ¼ teaspoon salt in a bowl to form a smooth paste. With the back of a spoon, rub the paste all over the lamb, then use your fingers to spread the paste evenly, making sure all the lamb is covered.

Put the lamb bone side down in a deep baking dish and place on the top shelf of the oven. Bake for 10 minutes, then baste the lamb and return it to the oven. Reduce the oven temperature to 160°C (315°F/Gas 2–3). Bake for 3¼ hours, basting every 20–30 minutes, to ensure the lamb stays tender and flavoursome.

Carve the lamb into chunky pieces. Mix the remaining cumin with the coarse salt and serve on the side for dipping.

Berber in origin, mechoui is spit-roasted lamb at its best. When Berbers have their moussems (festivals), the roasting of the lamb is the highlight of their celebrations. A mixture of spices (cumin, coriander and paprika), crushed garlic and salt is rubbed over the lamb and pushed into incisions, then the whole lamb is rubbed generously with herbed smen. Spit-roasted over a glowing charcoal fire, the lamb is frequently basted with the smen to keep it moist and succulent. The lamb is cooked until it is butter-soft so that morsels can be pulled off with the fingers. Cumin mixed with salt is the traditional accompaniment.

three ways with quince

QUINCE IS TEAMED WITH LAMB AND POULTRY FOR SWEET—SOUR DISHES OF PERSIAN ORIGIN; THE MOROCCAN VERSIONS ARE MORE HIGHLY SPICED. WHILE THE MOROCCANS DO NOT MAKE QUINCE PASTE, IT IS USED IN ONE OF THE RECIPES BELOW FOR THE FLAVOUR OF QUINCE OUT OF SEASON. POACHING QUINCE WITH THE SKIN AND CORE INTACT GIVES A ROSY HUE TO THE FRUIT, SOMETHING THAT IS OTHERWISE DIFFICULT TO ACHIEVE, UNLESS THE QUINCE IS SLOWLY COOKED FOR 2 HOURS OR MORE, BY WHICH TIME IT IS OVERCOOKED.

lamb tagine with quince

Cut 1.5 kg (3 lb 5 oz) lamb shoulder into 3 cm (1 1/4 in) pieces. Put the lamb in a heavy-based, flameproof casserole dish. Roughly chop 2 large handfuls coriander (cilantro) leaves and add to the dish, along with 1 diced large onion, 1/2 teaspoon ground ginger, 1/2 teaspoon cayenne pepper, 1/4 teaspoon ground saffron threads, 1 teaspoon ground coriander, 1 cinnamon stick and some salt and freshly ground black pepper. Cover with cold water and bring to the boil over medium heat. Lower the heat and simmer, partly covered, for 1 1/2 hours, or until the lamb is tender. While the lamb is cooking, peel, core and quarter 500 g (1 lb 2 oz) quinces. Melt 40 g (1 1/2 oz) butter in a heavy-based frying pan over medium heat and cook the quinces and 1 diced large onion for 15 minutes, or until lightly golden. When the lamb has been cooking for 1 hour, add the quince mixture, 100 g (3 1/2 oz/1/2 cup) dried apricots and 1 tablespoon caster (superfine) sugar. Taste the sauce and adjust the seasoning if necessary. Transfer to a warm serving dish and sprinkle with coriander (cilantro) leaves. Serve with couscous or rice. Serves 4–6.

chicken and quince tagine

You will need a 1.5 kg (3 lb 5 oz) chicken that has been cut into quarters. Cut diagonal slashes in the fleshy parts of the chicken pieces such as the breasts, legs and thighs. Rub 2 teaspoons ras el hanout into the chicken, cover and leave to marinate for 20 minutes. Heat 2 tablespoons oil in a large lidded frying pan over medium heat. Add the chicken pieces in batches, skin side down, and brown lightly for 2 minutes, then turn them over and cook for a further 2 minutes. Remove to a plate. Add 1 sliced onion to the pan and cook for 5 minutes, or until soft. Add 250 ml (9 fl oz/1 cup) chicken stock, stir well to lift the browned juices off the base of the pan, then return the chicken to the pan. Season lightly with salt if necessary. Reduce the heat to low, then cover and simmer for 45 minutes, turning the chicken occasionally. When the chicken is tender, cut 90 g (3 1/4 oz) quince paste into thin slices, then add it to the pan juices, mashing it with a fork until it melts into the liquid. Stir in 1 tablespoon lemon juice and 2 teaspoons rosewater and simmer for 1 minute. Serve the chicken with the quince sauce and spiced carrots (page 30). Serves 4.

poached quinces with rosewater

Wash 2 quinces well and cut into quarters. Place in a saucepan and cover with water. Bring to the boil, then cover and simmer over low heat for 40 minutes, or until almost tender and beginning to colour. Drain in a fine sieve over a bowl and return the liquid to the pan. Add 175 g (6 oz/3/4 cup) sugar and the thinly peeled zest of 1/2 lemon to the pan. Stir until the sugar has dissolved, then leave to simmer gently. Meanwhile, pull the skin from the quince quarters, remove the cores and halve each quarter. Place the quince slices in the syrup with 1 tablespoon rosewater. Simmer, uncovered, for a further 30 minutes, or until the quinces are tender and have a rosy hue. Remove the lemon zest and serve warm or chilled. Serves 4.

lamb with eggs and almonds .... serves 6

CALLED TAFAYA, THIS TAGINE IS SERVED AT CELEBRATIONS THROUGHOUT MOROCCO. TO GIVE THE DISH A FESTIVE TOUCH, SOME COOKS DIP THE SHELLED, BOILED EGGS IN SAFFRON-INFUSED HOT WATER, WHICH COLOURS THEM AND GIVES THEM EXTRA FLAVOUR.

lamb shoulder chops	1.25 kg (2 lb 12 oz)
olive oil	60 ml (2 fl oz/¼ cup)
onions	2, coarsely grated
garlic	3 cloves, finely chopped
ground ginger	2 teaspoons
ground saffron threads	¼ teaspoon
coriander (cilantro)	3 tablespoons chopped leaves, plus extra, to serve
butter	40 g (1½ oz)
blanched almonds	150 g (5½ oz/1 cup)
eggs	6, hard-boiled and halved

Trim the excess fat from the chops. Heat half the oil in a large saucepan over high heat and brown the lamb in batches, removing to a dish when cooked. Add a little more oil as required.

Reduce the heat to low, add the remaining oil and the onion and cook for 5 minutes, or until the onion has softened. Add the garlic and ginger and cook for a few seconds. Pour in 375 ml (13 fl oz/ 1½ cups) water and stir to lift the browned juices off the base of the pan. Return the lamb to the pan, along with the saffron, 1 teaspoon salt and a good grinding of black pepper. Cover and simmer over low heat for 1¼ hours, then stir in the coriander and cook for a further 15 minutes, or until the lamb is tender.

Meanwhile, melt the butter in a frying pan over medium heat and fry the almonds, tossing frequently, until golden. Remove immediately.

Arrange the lamb in a serving dish, spoon the sauce over and arrange the eggs on top. Sprinkle with the roasted almonds and extra coriander.

It takes the stigmas of 2000 blooms of the *Crocus sativus* to produce 10 grams (¼ oz) of dried saffron threads, making it the world's most expensive spice. Introduced by the Arabs via Moorish Spain, it is now grown, harvested and processed in Morocco. Threads and ground saffron are used for flavour and colour. The threads should be steeped in liquid before use, or added dry to tagines and soups during cooking. To make your own ground saffron, lightly roast the threads in a dry, heated frying pan and pound in a mortar with a pestle. Where a recipe calls for a pinch, use as much as sits on the very tip of a knife, as fingertips would take more than required.

almond-crusted fish with prunes .... serves 4

THE FRIED FISH STAYS MOIST AND SUCCULENT IN ITS DELICATELY FLAVOURED ALMOND CRUST. FISH BAKED WITH AN ALMOND CRUST IS A SPECIALITY OF THE COASTAL CITY OF SAFI. PRUNES ARE ALSO USED WITH FISH, AS A STUFFING OR IN A DELICIOUS SPICY SAUCE.

white fish fillets, such as blue eye cod, snapper, hake or sea bass	4 x 200 g (7 oz)
pitted prunes	24
blanched almonds	24, lightly roasted
butter	30 g (1 oz)
onions	2, sliced
ground ginger	3/4 teaspoon
ground cinnamon	3/4 teaspoon
freshly ground black pepper	1/8 teaspoon
ground saffron threads	1/8 teaspoon
sugar	1 1/2 teaspoons
lemon juice	3 teaspoons
orange flower water	3 teaspoons
egg	1
ground almonds	100 g (3 1/2 oz/1 cup)
smen or ghee	3–4 tablespoons
lemon wedges	to serve

Choose centre-cut fish fillets no more than 3 cm (1 1/4 in) thick at the thickest part. Remove the skin (if present) and season lightly with salt. Set aside. Stuff each prune with a whole roasted almond and set aside.

Melt the butter in a lidded frying pan and add the onion. Cook for about 10 minutes over low heat, stirring often, until the onion is soft and golden. Add 1/2 teaspoon each of the ground ginger and cinnamon, a pinch of salt and the black pepper. Stir and cook for a few seconds. Pour in 250 ml (9 fl oz/1 cup) water and stir in the saffron. Cover and simmer gently for 5 minutes, then add the stuffed prunes, sugar, lemon juice and orange flower water and stir gently. Cover and simmer for 15 minutes, or until the prunes are plump.

Meanwhile, beat the egg in a shallow dish with the remaining ground ginger and cinnamon and 1/4 teaspoon salt. Spread the ground almonds in a flat dish. Dip the fish into the beaten egg, drain briefly, and coat on all sides with the ground almonds. Place on a tray lined with baking paper.

Melt the smen or ghee in a large non-stick frying pan over medium to high heat (the depth of the smen should be about 5 mm/1/4 in). Add the coated fish, reduce the heat to medium and cook for 2 minutes, then turn and cook for a further 2 minutes, or until golden and just cooked through. Do not allow the almond coating to burn. If you have to remove the fish before it is cooked through, place it on top of the onion and prune mixture, cover and simmer gently for 2–3 minutes, taking care that the coating does not become too moist on top. Serve the fish immediately with lemon wedges, and the onion and prune sauce poured over.

Press a roasted almond into each of the prunes.

Dip the fish in the egg, then coat it with the ground almonds.

three ways with rice

RICE IS NOT WIDELY USED IN MAINSTREAM MOROCCAN COOKING APART FROM RICE PUDDING (PAGE 188) AND ITS VARIATIONS — SUCH AS USING THE THICK PUDDING AS A FILLING FOR FRIED BRIOUATS (SWEET PASTRIES SERVED AS A 'BREAK FAST' FOOD DURING RAMADAN). HOWEVER, IN TETUÁN, ONCE THE CAPITAL OF SPANISH MOROCCO, RICE FEATURES MORE FREQUENTLY. MOROCCANS USUALLY STEAM THE RICE IN THE SAME WAY AS COUSCOUS, ONLY COVERED — A VERY LENGTHY PROCESS.

saffron rice

Wash 500 g (1 lb 2 oz/2$\frac{1}{2}$ cups) long-grain rice in a sieve until the water runs clear, then drain well. Bring 875 ml (30 fl oz/3$\frac{1}{2}$ cups) water to the boil and add $\frac{1}{2}$ teaspoon crushed saffron threads. Allow to infuse for 20 minutes. Heat 2 tablespoons olive oil in a heavy-based saucepan and add the rice, stirring well so that all the rice is coated evenly in the oil. Add the saffron water and $\frac{1}{4}$ teaspoon salt and stir well. Bring to the boil and boil for 1 minute. Cover with a tight-fitting lid, then reduce the heat to as low as possible and cook for 10–12 minutes, or until all the water has been absorbed. Steam tunnels will form holes on the surface. Turn off the heat, then leave the pan covered for at least 10 minutes. Add 20 g ($\frac{3}{4}$ oz) butter, fluff lightly with a fork and serve. Serves 6.

rice stuffing for chicken

Cook 1 chopped onion in 2 tablespoons olive oil in a saucepan over medium heat until soft, about 5 minutes. Add 110 g (3$\frac{3}{4}$ oz/ $\frac{1}{2}$ cup) short-grain rice and cook, stirring occasionally, until the rice is opaque. Add 2 peeled, chopped tomatoes, 2 tablespoons chopped flat-leaf (Italian) parsley, 2 teaspoons chopped mint, $\frac{1}{2}$ teaspoon paprika, a pinch each of cayenne pepper and sugar and 375 ml (13 fl oz/1$\frac{1}{2}$ cups) chicken stock. Stir well and bring to the boil. Cover and simmer over low heat for 12 minutes, or until the rice is almost cooked and the liquid has been absorbed. When cool, use to stuff 2 chickens for roasting, packing the stuffing loosely. If only 1 chicken is cooked, stir a little more water into the remaining stuffing in the saucepan, cook over low heat until tender and serve with the chicken. Makes enough stuffing for 2 chickens.

silverbeet with rice

Trim the ends of the stalks of 900 g (2 lb) silverbeet (Swiss chard). Wash well and cut the stalks from the leaves. Slice the stalks thickly and roughly shred the leaves. Heat 80 ml (2$\frac{1}{2}$ fl oz/$\frac{1}{3}$ cup) olive oil in a large saucepan and add 1 chopped onion. Cook over low heat for 5 minutes, or until soft. Stir in the silverbeet stalks and 1 teaspoon paprika and cook for 5 minutes more. Add the silverbeet leaves, 2 tablespoons each of chopped coriander (cilantro) leaves and flat-leaf (Italian) parsley, 110 g (3$\frac{3}{4}$ oz/$\frac{1}{2}$ cup) short-grain rice and 125 ml (4 fl oz/$\frac{1}{2}$ cup) water. Increase the heat and stir until the silverbeet begins to wilt. Reduce the heat to low, add 1$\frac{1}{2}$ tablespoons lemon juice and stir well. Cover and simmer for 25 minutes, or until the rice is tender, stirring occasionally. Season, to taste, and serve hot as a vegetable accompaniment. Serves 4.

saffron rice

trout stuffed with dates .... serves 4

THE MARRIAGE OF DATES WITH FISH IS A TIME-HONOURED PRACTICE IN MOROCCO. TRADITIONALLY THE STUFFED FISH WOULD BE COOKED IN A TAGINE, BUT WITH DOMESTIC OVENS NOW MORE WIDELY AVAILABLE, IT IS OFTEN OVEN-BAKED. THE FOIL WRAPPING KEEPS THE FISH MOIST.

trout	4 medium
dates	140 g (5 oz/³/4 cup) chopped
rice	50 g (1³/4 oz/¹/4 cup) cooked
onion	1, finely chopped
coriander (cilantro)	4 tablespoons chopped leaves
ground ginger	¹/4 teaspoon
ground cinnamon	¹/4 teaspoon, plus extra, to serve
blanched almonds	50 g (1³/4 oz/¹/3 cup) roughly chopped
butter	40 g (1¹/2 oz), softened

Preheat the oven to 180°C (350°F/Gas 4). Rinse the trout under cold running water and pat them dry with paper towels. Season lightly with salt and freshly ground black pepper.

Combine the dates, cooked rice, half the onion, the coriander, ginger, cinnamon, almonds and half the butter in a bowl. Season well with salt and freshly ground black pepper.

Spoon the stuffing into the fish cavities and place each fish on a well-greased double sheet of foil. Brush the fish with the remaining butter, season with salt and freshly ground black pepper and divide the remaining onion among the four parcels. Wrap the fish neatly and seal the edges of the foil. Place the parcels on a large baking tray and bake for 15–20 minutes, or until cooked to your liking. Serve dusted with ground cinnamon.

While the coastal regions of Morocco benefit from a plentiful supply of seafood, inland dwellers depend on freshwater fish, as the freshness of ingredients is of paramount importance to cooks. Salmon (sea) trout and shad (alose) are two fish that enter the rivers from the Atlantic to spawn, with the shad regarded as better for eating at this stage. In Fez, fish, such as shad caught in the Sebou River, feature on banquet menus, baked with dates stuffed with a ground almond paste. Both shad and salmon trout have small bones, especially the shad, and care should be taken when eating; this is where eating with the hand is such an advantage, as it is easier to feel the bones.

fish with harissa and olives

THE SPICY TOMATO SAUCE TAKES ON QUITE A BITE WITH THE ADDITION OF HARISSA — ADD IT WITH CAUTION IF YOU HAVE NOT USED IT BEFORE. IF YOU DO NOT HAVE HARISSA, ADD 1 TEASPOON OF FINELY CHOPPED RED CHILLI OR A PINCH OF CAYENNE PEPPER. BESIDES THE TYPES GIVEN, OTHER SUITABLE FISH ARE HAKE AND SEA BASS.

plain (all-purpose) flour	for dusting
olive oil	80 ml (2¹/₂ fl oz/¹/₃ cup)
white fish fillets, such as blue eye cod, snapper or perch	4
onion	1, chopped
garlic	2 cloves, crushed
chopped tomatoes	400 g (14 oz) can
harissa	2 teaspoons, or to taste
bay leaves	2
cinnamon stick	1
black olives	175 g (6 oz/1 cup)
lemon juice	1 tablespoon
flat-leaf (Italian) parsley	2 tablespoons chopped

Season the flour with salt and freshly ground black pepper. Heat half the olive oil in a heavy-based frying pan. Dust the fish fillets with the seasoned flour and add to the pan. Cook the fish over medium heat for 2 minutes on each side, or until golden. Transfer to a plate.

Add the remaining olive oil to the pan and cook the onion and garlic for 3–4 minutes, or until softened. Add the tomatoes, harissa, bay leaves and cinnamon stick. Cook for 10 minutes, or until the sauce has thickened. Season, to taste, with salt and freshly ground black pepper.

Return the fish to the pan, add the olives and cover the fish with the sauce. Remove the bay leaves and cinnamon stick and cook for 2 minutes, or until the fish is tender. Add the lemon juice and parsley and serve.

Dust the fish fillets with the seasoned flour before cooking.

Cook the fish fillets over medium heat until golden.

COUSCOUS

Couscous and instant couscous both require steaming for best results. For 4–5 serves, put 325 g (11½ oz/1¾ cups) couscous in a large, shallow bowl and cover with water. Stir and pour the water off immediately through a strainer, returning the grains to the bowl. Leave for 15 minutes to swell, then rake with your fingers to separate the grains.

Line a steamer or couscoussier with two layers of cheesecloth, add the couscous and put the steamer over boiling stew or water, making sure the steamer does not touch the liquid. If it does not fit snugly, put a folded strip of foil between the steamer and the pan. Steam, uncovered, for 20 minutes, forking through the couscous occasionally. Turn into the bowl. Stir ½ teaspoon salt into 80 ml (2½ fl oz/⅓ cup) cold water. Add 30 g (1 oz) chopped butter to the couscous and sprinkle with the salted water. Toss through the couscous, and when cool enough, lightly rub handfuls of couscous to break up lumps. Cover and set aside. Twenty minutes before the stew is cooked, return the couscous to the lined steamer and replace over the boiling stew. Fluff up occasionally with a fork.

To cook in the microwave, put the swollen couscous in a 3 litre (104 fl oz) ceramic dish. Stir ½ teaspoon salt into 250 ml (9 fl oz/1 cup) water. Sprinkle a third of the water over the couscous, cover and microwave on full power for 3 minutes. Add 30 g (1 oz) chopped butter and fluff up with a fork. Repeat twice more with the remaining water and fluff with the fork each time. Uncover and fluff up again before serving.

couscous with lamb and raisins

THIS IS ONE OF THE SWEET COUSCOUS DISHES SERVED AT DIFFAS (BANQUETS), THE SWEETNESS COMING FROM THE ADDITION OF RICH-TASTING RAISINS. THE LAMB SHANK MEAT COOKS TO MELTING TENDERNESS, BUT OTHER LAMB CUTS CAN BE USED, SUCH AS THICKLY CUT SHOULDER CHOPS.

onions	3
butter	60 g (2^1/4 oz)
lamb shanks	3
ground turmeric	^{1}/2 teaspoon
ground ginger	1^1/2 teaspoons
freshly ground black pepper	1 teaspoon
ground saffron threads	^{1}/4 teaspoon
cayenne pepper	a pinch
coriander (cilantro)	3 sprigs
flat-leaf (Italian) parsley	3 sprigs
chickpeas	425 g (15 oz) can
raisins	90 g (3^1/4 oz/^{3}/4 cup)
couscous	1 quantity (page 140)

Quarter 2 of the onions. Halve and slice the remaining onion and set aside. Heat the butter in a large saucepan or the base of a large couscoussier. Add the lamb shanks, onion quarters, turmeric, ginger, black pepper, saffron and cayenne pepper and stir over low heat for 1 minute. Add 500 ml (17 fl oz/2 cups) water. Tie the coriander and parsley sprigs in a bunch and add to the pan with 1 teaspoon salt. Bring to a gentle boil, then cover and simmer over low heat for 1^3/4–2 hours, or until the lamb is very tender.

Meanwhile, drain the chickpeas and put them in a large bowl with cold water to cover. Lift up handfuls of chickpeas and rub them between your hands to loosen the skins. Run more water into the bowl, stir well and let the skins float to the top, then skim them off. Repeat until all the skins have been removed. Drain the chickpeas and set aside.

When the lamb is cooked, lift the shanks from the broth and strip off the meat. Discard the bones and cut the meat into pieces. Return the meat to the pan, along with the chickpeas, reserved onion and the raisins. Cover and cook for 20 minutes, adding a little more water to the pan if necessary.

Meanwhile, prepare and steam the couscous as directed, either over the stew or over a saucepan of boiling water, or in the microwave oven.

Pile the couscous on a large, warm platter and make a dent in the centre. Remove and discard the herbs, then ladle the lamb mixture into the hollow. Moisten with some of the broth and put the remaining broth in a bowl, which can be added as needed.

Rub the chickpeas between your hands to loosen the skins.

Strip the tender meat off the lamb shanks.

roast chicken with couscous stuffing

MOROCCAN COOKS USUALLY STEAM STUFFED CHICKEN OR COOK IT WHOLE IN A TAGINE. TO BROWN IT, THEY REMOVE IT FROM ITS SAUCE IF NECESSARY, AND FRY IT ON ALL SIDES IN A FRYING PAN. THE FOLLOWING RECIPE IS FOR OVEN-ROASTED CHICKEN.

chicken	1.6 kg (3 lb 8 oz)
paprika	2 teaspoons
butter	30 g (1 oz), softened
chicken stock	250 ml (9 fl oz/1 cup)

stuffing

couscous	140 g (5 oz/3/4 cup)
raisins	40 g (1 1/2 oz/1/3 cup)
butter	30 g (1 oz), diced
honey	1 tablespoon
ground cinnamon	1/2 teaspoon
blanched almonds	40 g (1 1/2 oz/1/4 cup), lightly roasted

Preheat the oven to 180°C (350°F/Gas 4). Rinse the cavity of the chicken and dry with paper towels. Season the chicken on the outside and sprinkle with the paprika. Rub it into the skin.

To make the stuffing, put the couscous in a glass or ceramic lidded casserole dish and mix in the raisins, butter, honey and cinnamon. Pour in 125 ml (4 fl oz/1/2 cup) boiling water, stir well and set aside until the water has been absorbed. Fluff up the grains with a fork to break up the lumps, cover and microwave on High (100%) for 2 1/2 minutes. Fluff up again with the fork, add the almonds and toss through. Alternatively, follow the directions on the packet to prepare the couscous, adding the extra ingredients.

Spoon half the stuffing into the cavity of the chicken, packing it in loosely. Tie the legs together and tuck the wing tips under.

Spread a little of the softened butter in the base of a baking dish. Put the chicken breast side up in the dish, spread with the remaining butter and pour the stock into the dish. Roast for 1 1/2–1 3/4 hours, basting often with the liquid in the baking dish. Remove to a platter and rest in a warm place for 15 minutes before carving. The cooking juices may be strained over the chicken. Reheat the remaining couscous stuffing and serve with the chicken, along with orange and date salad (page 120) or orange and carrot salad (page 30).

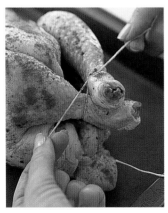

Pack the stuffing into the chicken and tie the legs together.

Roast the chicken until tender, basting with the cooking juices.

sweet couscous . . . . serves 4–6

COUSCOUS IS SERVED AS THE FINAL SAVOURY DISH OF A BANQUET AND A SWEET COUSCOUS IS OFTEN SERVED. AS IT IS A POPULAR DISH AT PALACE BANQUETS, THE MORE EXPENSIVE NUTS — PISTACHIOS AND PINE NUTS — ARE OFTEN USED ALONG WITH THE TRADITIONAL ALMONDS AND WALNUTS.

pistachio nuts, pine nuts and blanched almonds	80 g (2³/4 oz/1/2 cup) combined
dried apricots	50 g (1³/4 oz/1/4 cup)
couscous	250 g (9 oz/1¹/3 cups)
caster (superfine) sugar	55 g (1 oz/1/4 cup), plus 2 tablespoons, extra
unsalted butter	90 g (3¹/4 oz), softened
ground cinnamon	1/2 teaspoon
milk	375 ml (13 fl oz/1¹/2 cups) hot

Preheat the oven to 160°C (315°F/Gas 2–3). Spread the nuts on a baking tray and bake for about 5 minutes, or until lightly golden. Allow to cool, then coarsely chop and place in a bowl. Slice the apricots into matchstick-sized pieces. Add to the bowl with the nuts and toss to combine.

Put the couscous and sugar in a large bowl and cover with 250 ml (9 fl oz/1 cup) boiling water. Stir well, then add the butter and a pinch of salt. Stir until the butter melts. Cover with a tea towel and set aside for 10 minutes. (Alternatively, prepare and steam or microwave the couscous as described on page 140.) Fluff the grains with a fork, then toss through half the fruit and nut mixture.

To serve, pile the warm couscous in the centre of a platter. Arrange the remaining nut mixture around the edge. Combine the extra sugar and the cinnamon in a small bowl and serve separately for sprinkling. Pass around the hot milk in a jug for guests to help themselves.

While there are other members of the family Pistacia, *Pistacia vera*, native to Western Asia, is the species that produces the pistachio nut. The Romans introduced the pistachio tree to North Africa, but it has yet to rival the almond in popularity in Morocco. The fruit of the tree resembles green olives, with a reddish blush when ripe. When the outer covering is removed, the beige, smooth-shelled nut is already partly opened, exposing the kernel — in Iran, the most prolific producer of pistachios, this is termed khandan (smiling). The pistachio nut itself has the advantage of being green, or green-tinged, adding colour to dessert dishes and pastries as well as its delicate flavour.

sweets, pastries
and drinks

Moroccans prefer to complete a meal with fresh fruit, so there are very few traditional desserts or puddings. The only two of note served in the home are rice pudding and mulhalabia, an almond cream pudding. Yoghurt, of course, is another 'dessert', but the Moroccans only eat it mixed with sugar or honey — it is not used in other dishes. However, when fruit is served at banquets, some cooks are imaginative in their presentation, using orange flower water and rosewater to good effect, with a sprinkling of almonds, walnuts or mint leaves. Fresh figs, watermelon, oranges, bananas and peaches can look quite festive and the extra touches turn the fruit into tempting desserts.

Moroccan pastries have links to those of the Middle East, but are completely different in their final form. The ghoriba is a biscuit you will find from the Middle East to Morocco in various forms, but Moroccans make baklawa-type pastries their way — unique and just as delicious.

The similarities as far as pastries are concerned are in other ingredients used. Almonds feature prominently, especially ground almonds. Powdered sugar, cinnamon, orange flower water, rosewater, a hint of lemon zest, honey — these are the popular additives for making many of them. Walnuts, dates, dried figs, sesame seeds and, to a lesser extent, pistachio nuts are also used according to the whim of the cook or the art of the patissière.

Fruit and almonds also feature in sharbats, sublime concoctions mixed with milk. Almond sharbat, flavoured with rosewater, is one of the best; apple, raisin, strawberry and avocado sharbats are also made. Fruit juices (orange, grape, pomegranate and watermelon) are flavoured with the aromatic flower waters or a dusting of ground cinnamon — so Moroccan in concept. These drinks are of great importance as alcohol is forbidden by the Koran.

One beverage that was introduced from Arabia centuries ago is water perfumed with fragrant fumes. Grains of gum arabic are thrown on the embers of a charcoal brazier, an unglazed pottery water jug is inverted over the fragrant smoke and is impregnated with the fumes. When the porous jug is filled with water, the water cools by evaporation and absorbs the fragrance. Unfortunately, with the availability of bottled mineral water, few Moroccans prepare it today.

However, none of these beverages come even close to mint tea in popularity — its supremacy is assured.

honey-dipped briouats
with almond paste .... makes 18

THESE CRISP, HONEY-DIPPED PASTRIES ARE FILLED WITH A DELICIOUS ALMOND PASTE FRAGRANT WITH ORANGE FLOWER WATER. WHEN BOILING HONEY FOR DIPPING, IT IS IMPORTANT TO ADD WATER OTHERWISE THE HONEY BURNS. YOU MAY NEED TO ADD MORE WATER BEFORE DIPPING IS COMPLETED.

ground almonds	200 g (7 oz/2 cups)
unsalted butter	90 g (3¹/4 oz)
icing (confectioners') sugar	60 g (2¹/4 oz/¹/2 cup)
almond extract	¹/4 teaspoon
orange flower water	2 tablespoons
filo pastry	6 sheets
smen	125 g (4¹/2 oz), melted
honey	250 g (9 oz/³/4 cup)

Heat a heavy-based saucepan, add the ground almonds and stir constantly until lightly roasted — about 3–4 minutes. Tip immediately into a bowl, add the butter and stir until melted. When cool, add the icing sugar, almond extract and 1 tablespoon of the orange flower water. Mix thoroughly to a paste.

Stack the filo sheets on a cutting board with the longer side towards you and, with a ruler and sharp knife, measure and cut the filo into strips 12 cm (5 in) wide and 28–30 cm (11–12 in) long. Stack the strips in the folds of a dry tea towel or cover them with plastic wrap to prevent them from drying out. You will need 18 strips.

Place a filo strip on the work surface, brush half the length with the smen and fold it in half to give a strip 6 cm (2¹/2 in) wide. Brush over the top with the smen and place a heaped tablespoon of the almond filling towards the end of the strip. Fold the end diagonally across the filling so that the base lines up with the side of the strip, forming a triangle. Fold straight up once, then fold diagonally to the opposite side. Continue folding in the same manner to the end of the strip, trimming any excess pastry with scissors. Place seam side down on a lightly greased baking tray. Repeat with the remaining ingredients and when completed, brush the tops lightly with the smen.

Preheat the oven to 180°C (350°F/Gas 4). It is best to do this after the triangles are completed so that the kitchen remains cool during shaping. Bake the pastries for 20–25 minutes, or until puffed and lightly golden.

Combine the honey, 60 ml (2 fl oz/¹/4 cup) water and the remaining orange flower water in a 1.5 litre (52 fl oz/6 cup) saucepan. Just before the pastries are removed from the oven, bring the honey to the boil, and then reduce the heat to low. Put two hot pastries at a time in the boiling honey, leave for 20 seconds and then remove with two forks to a tray lined with baking paper. Dip the remaining pastries in the same way, placing them on the tray right side up. As the pastries are dipped, the honey boils up in the pan, so take care. Cool and serve on the day of baking.

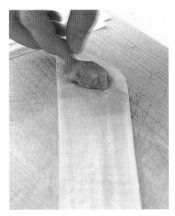
Fold the end of the filo over the filling to form a triangle.

Put the hot pastries in the boiling honey for 20 seconds.

fried honey cakes

WHILE YEAST DOUGHS ARE USUALLY PREPARED FOR SWEETS SUCH AS THESE DELICIOUS HONEY CAKES, HERE EGGS AND BAKING POWDER ARE USED TO GIVE THE DESIRED LIGHTNESS WITHOUT THE NEED FOR LENGTHY KNEADING OF THE DOUGH. ORANGE ZEST BOTH IN THE DOUGH AND THE HONEYED SYRUP LENDS A TRULY MOROCCAN FLAVOUR.

eggs	3
orange juice	60 ml (2 fl oz/¼ cup)
oil	60 ml (2 fl oz/¼ cup)
orange zest	1 tablespoon grated
caster (superfine) sugar	60 g (2¼ oz/¼ cup)
plain (all-purpose) flour	300 g (10½ oz/2⅓ cups), plus 40 g (1½ oz/⅓ cup), extra
baking powder	1 teaspoon
oil	for deep-frying

syrup

lemon juice	2 tablespoons
sugar	275 g (9¾ oz/1¼ cups)
honey	115 g (4 oz/⅓ cup)
orange zest	1 tablespoon grated

Whisk the eggs, orange juice and oil together in a large bowl. Add the orange zest and sugar and whisk until frothy. Sift in the flour and baking powder and mix with a wooden spoon until smooth, but still a bit sticky. Cover and set aside for 1 hour.

To make the syrup, put 300 ml (10½ fl oz) cold water with the lemon juice and sugar in a saucepan and heat, stirring until the sugar dissolves. Bring to the boil, then reduce the heat and simmer for 5 minutes. Add the honey and orange zest and simmer for a further 5 minutes. Keep warm.

Sprinkle a little of the extra flour onto the dough and transfer it to a lightly floured surface. Work in just enough extra flour to give a dough that doesn't stick to your hands. Roll it out to a thickness of 5 mm (¼ in). It will be very elastic, so keep rolling and resting it until it stops shrinking. Using a 5 cm (2 in) biscuit cutter, cut out round cakes.

Heat the oil in a large deep-sided frying pan to 170°C (325°F), or until a cube of bread dropped into the oil browns in 20 seconds. Fry the cakes three or four at a time for about 1 minute on each side, or until puffed and golden. Remove with tongs and drain on paper towels.

Using tongs, dip each cake into the warm honey syrup, long enough for it to soak in. Transfer to a platter. Serve warm or cold.

Fry the honey cakes until they are puffed and golden.

the desert date

According to a Moroccan saying, date palms must have their heads in fire and their feet in water — the hot Moroccan sun to bring the fruit to succulent sweetness, and ground water for their roots.

The date has sustained the desert nomads for countless centuries. It still sustains those who have not given up their traditional existence, and is just as important to villagers and city dwellers. For food on the move, the date is difficult to beat — an instant boost of energy with its high sugar content, and a little protein, vitamins and minerals thrown in. Taking a year to mature, fresh dates make their appearance in the souks in December, arranged painstakingly in mini pyramids. Hues vary from light golden brown, through red-brown to a rich chocolate. There are dates ready for eating immediately, dates for cooking and dates to have on hand for snacking.

As well as its fruit, the date palm provides fronds, which are dried and used for baskets and table mats. The fibre from its bark is made into ropes, the stones of the fruit are used for fuel and the trunk is used for timber. Date palms can produce fruit for 60 years; however, they can exceed 30 metres (100 feet) in height and are cut down when harvesting becomes too difficult. In the Erfoud oasis alone, one million date palms flourish, encompassing 30 varieties. The average annual yield is about 45 kg (100 lb) of fruit per tree.

Muslims regard the date palm as the tree of life and it is easy to see why.

sesame biscuits .... makes about 36

SESAME SEEDS STAR IN THESE DELICIOUS BISCUITS. THEIR NUTTY FLAVOUR IS ACCENTUATED WHEN ROASTED, BUT TAKE CARE THAT THE SEEDS DO NOT BURN. THEY CAN BE BOUGHT FROM PATISSERIES IN THE CITIES, TO BE TAKEN HOME OR TO A NEARBY CAFÉ TO ENJOY WITH MINT TEA OR COFFEE.

sesame seeds	225 g (8 oz/1 1/2 cups), plus 2–3 tablespoons, extra
plain (all-purpose) flour	125 g (4 1/2 oz/1 cup) sifted
caster (superfine) sugar	175 g (6 oz/3/4 cup)
baking powder	1 1/2 teaspoons
eggs	2, beaten
orange flower water	1 tablespoon

Put the sesame seeds in a heavy-based saucepan and stir constantly over medium heat for about 7 minutes, or until golden. Tip them immediately into a bowl and leave to cool. Put the flour in the same saucepan, stir constantly over medium heat for about 5 minutes, or until lightly golden, then transfer immediately to a mixing bowl.

When the sesame seeds are cool, put them in a blender and process until reduced almost to a powder (this is best done in two batches as it is difficult to process the seeds efficiently in one batch). Some seeds should remain visible after processing. Add to the flour, along with the sugar and baking powder and mix thoroughly. Make a well in the centre and add the beaten eggs and orange flower water. Stir into the dry ingredients, then knead well until smooth.

Put the extra sesame seeds in a shallow dish. Line two baking trays with baking paper or grease them well with butter. Preheat the oven to 180°C (350°F/Gas 4).

Break off pieces of dough the size of a walnut and roll it into balls, oiling your hands lightly to prevent the dough from sticking. Press the balls in the sesame seeds and flatten slightly. Lift carefully so that the topping is not disturbed and place them sesame side up on the baking trays, spacing them 5 cm (2 in) apart to allow for spreading. Bake for 15–20 minutes, or until golden. Leave on the trays for 10 minutes before removing to a wire rack to cool. Store in an airtight container.

Stir the sesame seeds over medium heat until golden.

gazelle's horns

THESE PRETTY ALMOND-FILLED PASTRIES ARE CALLED KAAB EL GHZAL. FOR A DIFFERENT FINISH, THEY ARE ALSO DIPPED, ONE AT A TIME WHILE HOT, INTO A BOWL OF ORANGE FLOWER WATER, THEN INTO ANOTHER BOWL OF POWDERED SUGAR.

pastry

plain (all-purpose) flour	300 g (10½ oz/2½ cups)
butter	20 g (¾ oz), melted
egg yolk	1
orange flower water	2 tablespoons

almond filling

ground almonds	300 g (10½ oz/3 cups)
icing (confectioners') sugar	90 g (3¼ oz/¾ cup)
orange flower water	1 tablespoon
egg white	1, lightly beaten
unsalted butter	40 g (1½ oz), melted
ground cinnamon	½ teaspoon
almond extract	¼ teaspoon
icing (confectioners') sugar	to serve

To make the pastry, put the flour, butter, egg yolk, orange flower water and 60 ml (2 fl oz/¼ cup) cold water in a food processor. Process until the dough forms on the blades, adding a little more water if necessary. Process for 1 minute to make the dough elastic. Turn out onto the work surface and knead until smooth. Divide in half, wrap in plastic wrap and rest for 20 minutes.

To make the almond filling, mix all the ingredients to form a stiff paste. Shape the filling into 30 balls, using 3 teaspoons of filling in each. Oil your hands and roll each ball to form a torpedo shape 7.5 cm (3 in) long, tapering slightly at each end. Place on baking paper and set aside. Preheat the oven to 180°C (350°F/Gas 4).

Roll out one ball of dough on a lightly floured work surface to a 30 x 40 cm (12 x 16 in) rectangle, with the longer side facing you. Lay three almond shapes across the pastry, 5 cm (2 in) from the bottom edge, 3 cm (1¼ in) from the sides and about 5 cm (2 in) apart. Lightly brush the pastry edge and between the filling with water. Turn the bottom edge of the pastry over the filling and press firmly around the filling to seal. Cut around the filling with a fluted pastry wheel, leaving a 2 cm (¾ in) border. Place on a baking tray and gently bend upwards on the filling side to form a crescent. Straighten the edge of the pastry with a knife and repeat this process until all the filling is used (reroll the pastry trimmings). Bake for 15 minutes, or until lightly coloured. Transfer to a wire rack and dust with sifted icing sugar while hot.

Trim the edge of the pastry to give a straight edge.

Turn the bottom edge of the pastry over the almond shapes.

Use a pastry wheel to cut around the filling, leaving a border.

three ways with figs

ONE OF THE PLEASURES OF LATE SUMMER THROUGH AUTUMN WOULD HAVE TO BE EATING FRESH FIGS, PLUMP, PURPLE AND LUSCIOUS. IN LATE AUTUMN, THE GREEN OR WINTER FIGS ARE JUST AS DELICIOUS. MOROCCANS MAKE THE MOST OF FIGS IN SEASON, SERVING THEM AT THE END OF A MEAL, AND USE DRIED FIGS FOR SNACKING OR ADDING TO SWEET PASTRIES. WHILE YOGHURT IS NOT USUALLY SERVED WITH FRUIT (MOROCCANS EAT IT SWEETENED WITH SUGAR OR HONEY), ITS SLIGHT TARTNESS COMPLEMENTS THE SWEETNESS OF FIGS.

figs with rosewater, almonds and honey

Wash 12 fresh purple-skinned figs gently and pat them dry with paper towels. Cut each fig into quarters, starting from the stem end and cutting almost to the base, then gently open out and put on a serving platter. Cover and chill in the refrigerator for 1 hour, or until required. Coarsely chop 50 g (1³⁄4 oz/¹⁄3 cup) lightly roasted blanched almonds. Carefully dribble about ¹⁄4 teaspoon rosewater onto the exposed centre of each fig, and sprinkle 1 teaspoon of the chopped almonds into each fig. Drizzle 1–2 tablespoons honey over the nuts. Serve immediately. Serves 6.

poached figs with almonds and spices

Rinse 375 g (13 oz/2¹⁄3 cups) dried figs and place in a bowl with cold water to cover generously. Soak for 8 hours, or until plump. Drain the soaking water into a saucepan. Insert a blanched almond into each fig from the base. Wrap 3 cloves, 3 bruised cardamom pods and ¹⁄2 teaspoon black peppercorns in a piece of muslin and tie securely. Add 115 g (4 oz/¹⁄2 cup) sugar to the soaking liquid and cook over medium heat, stirring, until the sugar has dissolved. Bring to the boil, add the bag of spices, the thinly peeled zest of ¹⁄2 lemon, 1 cinnamon stick and the figs. Return to the boil, then reduce the heat and simmer for 30 minutes, or until tender. Transfer the figs to a serving dish with a slotted spoon and strain the syrup over them. Serve warm or chilled with thick yoghurt. Serves 4–6.

figs with honeyed yoghurt

Gently wash 12 fresh figs and dry gently with paper towels. Chill for 30 minutes. Mix 250 g (9 oz/1 cup) thick Greek-style yoghurt with 2 tablespoons honey. Coarsely chop 2 tablespoons pistachio nuts and set aside. Cut each fig into quarters, starting from the stem end and cutting almost to the base. Gently open each fig and place on a flat serving dish. Dribble ¹⁄4 teaspoon orange flower water over the exposed centre of each fig and pile about 1 tablespoon of the yoghurt into each. Drizzle 1 teaspoon honey on top of the yoghurt in each fig and sprinkle with the chopped pistachios. Serves 4–6.

figs with rosewater, almonds and honey

ghoriba . . . . makes about 50

GHORIBA ARE BAKED FROM THE MIDDLE EAST TO MOROCCO. INGREDIENTS VARY A LITTLE; THIS MOROCCAN VERSION USES VERY FINE SEMOLINA AS WELL AS FLOUR, BUT YOU CAN USE ALL FLOUR IF THE REQUIRED SEMOLINA IS UNAVAILABLE.

unsalted butter	250 g (9 oz)
plain (all-purpose) flour	125 g (4½ oz/1 cup)
icing (confectioners') sugar	125 g (4½ oz/1 cup), plus extra, to serve, optional
very fine semolina	300 g (10½ oz/2 cups)
eggs	2, beaten
natural vanilla extract	1 teaspoon
egg white	1, lightly beaten
blanched almonds	30 g (1 oz/¼ cup), split

Melt the butter in a heavy-based saucepan over low heat. Skim off the froth, then pour into a mixing bowl, leaving the white milk solids in the pan. Set aside to cool.

Sift the flour and icing sugar into a bowl, add the semolina and a pinch of salt and mix thoroughly. When the butter is cool but still liquid, stir in the egg and vanilla. Add the dry ingredients and mix to a firm dough, adding more flour if necessary. Knead well, then cover with plastic wrap and leave for 1 hour. Line two baking trays with baking paper. Preheat the oven to 180°C (350°F/Gas 4).

Knead the dough again until smooth and pliant. Take 3 level teaspoons of dough and shape into a smooth ball, then shape the remaining dough into balls of the same size. Place on the prepared trays 2.5 cm (1 in) apart. Brush the tops lightly with egg white and press an almond on top of each biscuit. Bake for 20 minutes, or until lightly golden. Cool on the trays. When cold, dust the biscuits with sifted icing sugar, if using, and store in an airtight container.

Semolina is the milled inner endosperm of hard or durum wheat, pale beige or yellow in colour and granular in appearance. It can be very fine (almost like a flour), fine or coarse, the latter used in the manufacture of couscous, although fine semolina is also used for a fine-grained couscous not readily available outside Morocco. Both fine and coarse semolina are sold as breakfast cereals, also called cream of wheat. Very fine semolina is available at markets selling Middle Eastern and Greek foods. Semolina flour, used in pasta making, is durum wheat flour and should not be confused with the semolina described above.

almond macaroons . . . . makes 30–35

THESE ALMOND BISCUITS ARE DIPPED INTO POWDERED SUGAR BEFORE BAKING. DURING BAKING, THEY RISE A LITTLE AND THE SUGAR TOPPING DEVELOPS A LOVELY CRACKED APPEARANCE. MOROCCAN COOKS TAKE THESE BISCUITS TO THE COMMUNAL OVEN FOR BAKING, TO BE ENJOYED LATER WITH MINT TEA.

ground almonds	300 g (10^1/$_2$ oz/3 cups)
icing (confectioners') sugar	150 g (5^1/$_2$ oz/1^1/$_4$ cups), plus
	30 g (1 oz/^{1}/$_4$ cup), extra
baking powder	1^1/$_2$ teaspoons
ground cinnamon	^{1}/$_2$ teaspoon
egg	1
lemon zest	2 teaspoons grated
rosewater	1 tablespoon

Put the ground almonds in a mixing bowl and sift in the icing sugar, baking powder and cinnamon. Stir well to mix the dry ingredients thoroughly. Beat the egg with the lemon zest and rosewater and add to the dry ingredients. Mix to a firm paste and knead lightly.

Line two baking trays with baking paper. Sift the extra icing sugar into a shallow dish. Preheat the oven to 180°C (350°F/Gas 4).

Break off pieces of dough the size of a walnut and roll into balls, oiling your hands lightly to prevent the dough sticking. Press the balls into the icing sugar and flatten them slightly. Lift carefully so that the topping is not disturbed, and place on the baking trays sugar side up, spacing them about 5 cm (2 in) apart to allow for spreading. Bake for 20 minutes. Leave the macaroons on the trays for 10 minutes before removing to a wire rack to cool. Store in an airtight container.

Mix the almond mixture to a firm paste and lightly knead it.

Press the balls of dough into the icing sugar.

three ways with flower waters

ONE OF THE DEFINING CHARACTERISTICS OF MOROCCAN COOKING IS THE USE OF FRAGRANT WATERS IN SAVOURY AND SWEET DISHES. KNOWN AS MA'EL WARD, ROSEWATER IS A DISTILLATION OF ROSE PETALS AND ORIGINATED IN PERSIA; IN MOROCCO, IT IS DISTILLED FROM ROSEBUDS COLLECTED IN THE VALLEY OF DADES. ORANGE FLOWER WATER IS KNOWN AS ZHAAR, AND IS A DISTILLATION OF THE BLOSSOMS OF THE BITTER BIGARADE OR SEVILLE ORANGE; IT ORIGINATED IN THE MIDDLE EAST. BOTH WATERS WERE INTRODUCED TO MOROCCO BY THE ARABS.

grape juice with rosewater

Wash 500 g (1 lb 2 oz) chilled seedless purple or green grapes very well, drain, then cut off the thicker stalks, leaving the grapes in small bunches. Feed the grapes into a juice extractor, catching the juice in a jug. When all the grapes are juiced, let the juice settle and then skim off any dark froth (this is the remnants of the stems and seeds). Cover the jug with plastic wrap and chill in the refrigerator for at least 1 hour. Decant the juice into 2 tall glasses, leaving any sediment in the jug. Stir ½ teaspoon rosewater into each glass and dust the top lightly with ground cinnamon, if desired. Serves 2.

watermelon juice with rosewater

Chill 800 g (1 lb 12 oz) watermelon thoroughly. Remove the rind and cut the pink part only into thick chunks that will fit into a juice extractor feed tube. Extract the juice into a jug. Take care when extracting the juice, as the seeds have a tendency to jump out of the feed tube. Add 1 teaspoon rosewater and pour into 2 tall glasses, or store in the jug in the refrigerator until ready to serve. Serves 2.

orange juice with orange flower water

Choose 6 sweet oranges and store them in the refrigerator so they are well chilled. Using a citrus juicer, juice the oranges, then pour the juice through a sieve into a jug. Stir in caster (superfine) sugar, to taste (you may not need to add any sugar at all if the oranges are very sweet), and add 1½ teaspoons orange flower water. Pour into 2 tall glasses and lightly dust the top with ground cinnamon, if desired. Serve immediately. Serves 2.

almond filo snake . . . . serves 8

M'HANNCHA IN MOROCCAN, THIS COILED PASTRY WITH ITS FRAGRANT ALMOND FILLING IS ONE OF MOROCCO'S MOST FAMOUS PASTRIES. SERVE IT IN WEDGES, OR AS THEY DO IN MOROCCO, BREAK OFF PIECES FROM THE COIL. EITHER WAY, ACCOMPANY WITH MINT TEA OR COFFEE.

egg	1 small, separated
ground almonds	200 g (7 oz/2 cups)
flaked almonds	30 g (1 oz/^{1}/3 cup)
icing (confectioners') sugar	125 g (4^1/2 oz/1 cup), plus extra, to serve
lemon zest	1 teaspoon finely grated
almond extract	^{1}/4 teaspoon
rosewater	1 tablespoon
unsalted butter or smen	90 g (3^1/4 oz), melted
filo pastry	8–9 sheets
ground cinnamon	a pinch

Preheat the oven to 180°C (350°F/Gas 4). Lightly grease a 20 cm (8 in) round springform tin.

Put the egg white in a bowl and beat lightly with a fork. Add the ground almonds, flaked almonds, icing sugar, lemon zest, almond extract and rosewater. Mix to a paste.

Divide the almond mixture into four and roll each portion on a cutting board into a sausage shape about 1 cm (1/2 in) thick and about 5 cm (2 in) shorter than the length of the filo (about 38 cm/15 in) long). If the paste is too sticky to roll, dust the board with icing sugar.

Keep the melted butter or smen warm by placing the saucepan in another pan filled with hot water. Remove one sheet of filo pastry and place the rest in the folds of a dry tea towel or cover them with plastic wrap to prevent them from drying out. Brush the filo sheet with the butter, then cover with another sheet, brushing the top with butter. Ease one almond 'sausage' off the board onto the buttered pastry, laying it along the length of the pastry, 2.5 cm (1 in) from the base and sides. Roll up to enclose the filling. Form into a coil and sit the coil seam side down in the centre of the prepared tin, tucking under the unfilled ends of the pastry to enclose the filling. Continue in this manner to make more pastry 'snakes', shaping to make a large coil. If the coil breaks, cut small pieces of the remaining filo sheet, brush with a little egg yolk and press the filo onto the breaks.

Add the cinnamon to the remaining egg yolk and brush over the coil. Bake for 30–35 minutes, or until golden brown. Dust with the extra icing sugar and serve warm. This sweet pastry can be stored at room temperature for up to two days.

Roll the filo pastry around the almond filling.

Fit the coils into the tin, tucking under the ends.

keneffa . . . . serves 6

IN MOROCCO, FRIED WARKHA PASTRY IS USED FOR THIS TRADITIONAL DESSERT. ASSEMBLED IN A STACK OF LARGE ROUNDS LAYERED WITH ALMOND CREAM AND ALMONDS, IT COLLAPSES INTO A CRUMBLED MASS ONCE PORTIONS ARE TAKEN FROM IT. MAKING INDIVIDUAL PASTRY STACKS USING WON TON WRAPPERS SOLVES THIS PROBLEM.

almond cream

full cream milk	750 ml (26 fl oz/3 cups)
cornflour (cornstarch)	35 g (1 1/4 oz/ 1/4 cup)
sugar	60 g (2 1/4 oz/ 1/4 cup)
ground almonds	50 g (1 3/4 oz/ 1/2 cup)
almond extract	1/4 teaspoon
rosewater	1 1/2 tablespoons
blanched almonds	100 g (3 1/2 oz/ 2/3 cup), lightly roasted
icing (confectioners') sugar	2 tablespoons, sifted, plus extra, to serve
ground cinnamon	1/2 teaspoon
square won ton wrappers	40
oil	for frying
organic rose petals	to serve

To make the almond cream, put 125 ml (4 fl oz/1/2 cup) of the milk in a large bowl, add the cornflour and mix to a thin paste. Bring the remaining milk to the boil until it froths up. Mix the cornflour paste again, then add the boiling milk, mixing constantly with a balloon whisk. Pour this back into the saucepan and stir in the sugar and ground almonds. Return to the heat and stir constantly with a wooden spoon until thickened and bubbling. Reduce the heat and boil gently for 1 minute. Pour the liquid back into the bowl and stir in the almond extract and rosewater. Press a piece of plastic wrap on the surface and leave to cool. Just before using the cream, stir briskly with a balloon whisk to smooth it; if it is too thick, stir in a little milk to give a pouring consistency.

Coarsely chop the roasted almonds, mix with the icing sugar and cinnamon and set aside.

Bring the won ton wrappers to room temperature. Lightly brush a wrapper with water and press another firmly on top. Repeat until there are 18 pairs. Make two extra pairs in case some are burnt during frying.

In a large frying pan, add oil to a depth of 1 cm (1/2 in) and place over high heat. When the oil is hot, but not smoking, reduce the heat to medium and add two pairs of won ton wrappers. Fry quickly for about 20 seconds until lightly browned, turning to brown evenly. Using tongs, remove the wrappers and drain on paper towels. Repeat with the remaining squares.

To assemble the pastries, put a fried pastry square in the centre of each plate. Drizzle with a little almond cream and sprinkle with a heaped teaspoon of the chopped almond mixture. Repeat with another pastry square, cream and almonds. Finish with another pastry square. Scatter with pink rose petals from roses that have not been sprayed. Sift a little icing sugar over the top and serve with the remaining almond cream in a jug.

Brush a wrapper with water and then press another on top.

Fry the pairs of won ton wrappers until lightly browned.

three ways with almonds

ALMONDS GROW PROLIFICALLY IN MOROCCO, AND SO ARE WIDELY USED IN COOKING. THE BLANCHED NUTS ARE ROASTED AND SCATTERED OVER TAGINES, POUNDED AND MADE INTO FRAGRANT PASTES FOR PASTRY FILLINGS, ADDED TO DESSERTS SUCH AS MULHALABIA (ALMOND CREAM PUDDING) AND MADE INTO A LIP-SMACKING SHARBAT BIL LOOZ (ALMOND SHARBAT). IN THE SOUTH, AMALOU (ALMOND AND HONEY SPREAD) IS A DELICIOUS SPREAD FOR BREAD OR PANCAKES. ARGAN OIL, FROM THE ARGAN TREE, IS TRADITIONALLY USED, BUT OTHER NUT OILS ARE FINE.

almond sharbat

Put 235 g (8$\frac{1}{2}$ oz/1$\frac{1}{2}$ cups) blanched almonds and 55 g (2 oz/$\frac{1}{4}$ cup) caster (superfine) sugar in a blender with 250 ml (9 fl oz/ 1 cup) water. Blend until the almonds are well pulverized. Line a strainer with a double layer of cheesecloth, place over a bowl and pour the almond mixture into the strainer. Add 60 ml (2 fl oz/$\frac{1}{4}$ cup) water to the blender and blend briefly to clean the blender of any almond residue. Pour into the strainer. Press the almonds to extract as much moisture as possible, gather up the cheesecloth, twist the end and squeeze firmly over the bowl, taking care that the almonds are safely enclosed. Put the cheesecloth and almonds in the strainer again, add another 60 ml (2 fl oz/$\frac{1}{4}$ cup) water, stir and squeeze the almonds again. Discard the almonds. Stir in $\frac{1}{4}$ teaspoon almond extract, $\frac{1}{2}$ teaspoon rosewater and 250 ml (9 fl oz/1 cup) milk, taste and add a little more sugar if necessary. Chill and serve. (If you can find them, float a fragrant pink rose petal or two on top of each, but ensure the petals are free of pesticides.) Serves 4.

almond cream pudding

Put 500 ml (17 fl oz/2 cups) milk and 55 g (2 oz/$\frac{1}{4}$ cup) caster (superfine) sugar in a heavy-based saucepan and heat over medium heat until the sugar has dissolved. Bring to the boil. In a large bowl, mix 2 tablespoons cornflour (cornstarch), 1 tablespoon ground rice and 60 ml (2 fl oz/$\frac{1}{4}$ cup) water to a smooth paste. Pour in the boiling milk, stirring constantly with a balloon whisk. Return to the saucepan and stir over medium heat until thickened and bubbling. Add 70 g (2$\frac{1}{2}$ oz/$\frac{2}{3}$ cup) ground almonds and simmer over low heat for 5 minutes, stirring occasionally. Add 1 teaspoon rosewater and remove the pan from the heat. Stir occasionally to cool a little, then spoon into serving bowls. Refrigerate for 1 hour. Mix 2 tablespoons roasted, slivered (or flaked) almonds with 1 teaspoon caster (superfine) sugar and $\frac{1}{2}$ teaspoon ground cinnamon and sprinkle over the top before serving. Serves 4.

almond and honey spread

Put 100 g (3$\frac{1}{2}$ oz/1 cup) ground almonds, a pinch of salt and 2 tablespoons walnut or macadamia nut oil in a bowl and stir well. Mix in 1 tablespoon dark honey and 3–4 drops almond extract. The amalou should have a soft, spreading consistency; if necessary, stir in a little more oil. The amount of oil required depends on how moist the ground almonds are. Serve the spread on bread, beghrir (semolina pancakes, page 176) or other pancakes, with additional honey if desired. The amalou can be stored in a sealed jar in the refrigerator for 3–4 weeks; bring to room temperature before serving. Makes 140 g (5 oz/$\frac{1}{2}$ cup).

almond sharbat

semolina pancakes

THE RESEMBLANCE TO ENGLISH CRUMPETS IS APPARENT, BUT ONCE TASTED, THERE IS NO COMPARISON. THESE LIGHT-AS-AIR PANCAKES ARE MADE WITH FLOUR AND VERY FINE SEMOLINA, RESULTING IN PANCAKES THAT BEG FOR LASHINGS OF BUTTER AND HONEY.

active dried yeast	1 tablespoon
plain (all-purpose) flour	250 g (9 oz/2 cups)
very fine semolina	250 g (9 oz/1²/₃ cups)
eggs	2
milk	125 ml (4 fl oz/¹/₂ cup) lukewarm
oil	for cooking
unsalted butter	to serve
honey	warm, to serve

Dissolve the yeast in 125 ml (4 fl oz/¹/₂ cup) lukewarm water and mix in 3 teaspoons of the flour. Cover with a cloth and leave in a warm place for 15 minutes until frothy.

Sift the remaining flour, semolina and ¹/₂ teaspoon salt into a mixing bowl and make a well in the centre. Beat the eggs lightly with the lukewarm milk and pour into the flour mixture, then add the yeast mixture and 375 ml (13 fl oz/1¹/₂ cups) lukewarm water. Starting with the flour surrounding the well and working outwards, bring the flour into the liquid, then beat well with a balloon whisk for 5–7 minutes until smooth, adding more water if necessary. The batter should have the consistency of thick cream. Cover the bowl with a folded tea towel and leave in a warm place for 1 hour until doubled in bulk and bubbles form.

Fill a saucepan one-third full with water, bring to a simmer, then place a large heatproof plate over the top. Put a tea towel, folded in quarters, on the plate.

Heat a heavy cast-iron frying pan or crepe pan over high heat. Reduce the heat to medium and rub the pan with a wad of paper towels dipped in oil. Pour in a small ladleful of batter, about 60 ml (2 fl oz/¹/₄ cup), and, using the bottom of the ladle, quickly shape into a round about 15 cm (6 in) in diameter. Work quickly and try to make the top as even as possible. Cook until the top of the pancake looks dry and is peppered with little holes from the bubbles. While it is not traditional, you can turn it over and briefly brown the bubbly side.

Remove the pancake to the folds of the tea towel, bubbly side up, and cover to keep warm. Overlap the pancakes rather than stack them. Repeat with the remaining batter, oiling the pan with the wad of paper towels between each pancake. Serve the pancakes hot with butter and warm honey.

Use the bottom of the ladle to shape the batter into a round.

Cook the pancake until the top is peppered with little holes.

moroccan doughnuts..makes 20

ALL OVER MOROCCO YOU WILL FIND DOUGHNUT MAKERS, WITH CAULDRONS OF HOT OIL, FRYING DOUGHNUTS TO ORDER. THESE ARE STRUNG ON LENGTHS OF PALM FROND AND TIED, TO BE TAKEN HOME OR TO A CAFÉ, WHERE THEY WILL BE DIPPED IN SUGAR AND ENJOYED WITH MINT TEA.

active dried yeast	2 teaspoons
sugar	1/2 teaspoon
plain (all-purpose) flour	375 g (13 oz/3 cups)
oil	for deep-frying
caster (superfine) sugar	to serve
ground cinnamon	to serve, optional

Dissolve the yeast in 125 ml (4 fl oz/1/2 cup) lukewarm water and stir in the sugar. Combine the flour and 1/2 teaspoon salt in a shallow mixing bowl and make a well in the centre. Pour the yeast mixture into the well and add another 125 ml (4 fl oz/1/2 cup) lukewarm water. Stir sufficient flour into the liquid to form a thin batter, cover the bowl with a cloth and leave for 15 minutes until bubbles form. Gradually stir in the remaining flour, then mix with your hand to form a soft dough. If it is too stiff, add a little more water, 1 teaspoon at a time. Knead for 5 minutes in the bowl until smooth and elastic. Pour a little oil down the side of the bowl, turn the dough to coat with oil, cover with a cloth and leave for 1 hour until doubled in bulk.

Punch down the dough, then turn it out onto the work surface and divide into 20 even-sized portions. With lightly oiled hands, roll each into a smooth ball. Brush a baking tray with oil. Using your index finger, punch a hole in the centre of one dough ball, then twirl it on your finger until the hole enlarges to 2 cm (3/4 in) in diameter. Place on the tray. Repeat with the remaining balls.

Fill a large saucepan one-third full of oil and heat to 190°C (375°F), or until a cube of bread dropped in the oil browns in 10 seconds. Have a long metal skewer on hand and begin with the first doughnut that was shaped. Drop the doughnut into the oil, immediately put the skewer in the centre, and twirl it around in a circular motion for 2–3 seconds to keep the hole open. Fry for 1 1/2–2 minutes, or until the doughnut is evenly browned. Once this process is mastered, drop 2–3 doughnuts at a time into the oil, briefly twirling the skewer in the centre of the first before adding the next. When cooked, put the skewer in the doughnut hole and lift it out onto a tray lined with paper towels.

Toss the doughnuts in sugar and eat while hot with coffee or mint tea. While it is not traditional in Morocco, cinnamon may be mixed with the sugar.

Twirl the doughnut in a circular motion to keep the hole open.

three ways with fresh fruit

IN EVERY MOROCCAN HOUSEHOLD, THE MAIN MEAL IS COMPLETED WITH FRESH FRUIT, EITHER PICKED FROM COURTYARD FRUIT TREES OR BOUGHT AT THE SOUK. AT BANQUETS, BEAUTIFULLY ARRANGED PLATTERS OF FRESH FRUIT, OFTEN NESTLED IN ICE, CELEBRATE THE SEASON. WHEN FRUIT IS PREPARED, IT COULD BE SCENTED WITH FLOWER WATER, DUSTED WITH CINNAMON, CROWNED WITH CHOPPED NUTS — A VISUAL AND SENSORY DELIGHT AND THE PERFECT FINALE TO A MEAL.

watermelon with rosewater and mint

Wipe the skin of a 1.5 kg (3 lb 5 oz) piece of watermelon with a clean, damp cloth. Working over a plate to catch any juice, remove the skin and cut the watermelon into 3 cm (1 1/4 in) cubes, removing any visible seeds. Pile the cubes in a bowl or on a platter. Pour the watermelon juice into a small jug and stir in 3 teaspoons rosewater. Sprinkle over the watermelon, cover and chill in the refrigerator for 1 hour, or until required. Scatter with small fresh mint leaves and serve chilled. Serves 4.

peaches with sugar and cinnamon

Peel 6 freestone peaches. To do this, cut around each peach following the groove on the side of the peach. Put the peaches in a bowl of boiling water for 1 minute, then plunge them into a bowl of cold water to cool. Remove from the water and peel the skin away — it should slip off easily. Separate the peach halves with a gentle twist and remove the stones. Brush the cut surfaces lightly with lemon juice. Sit the peach halves on a bed of crushed ice in a large, shallow bowl. Crush 4 sugar cubes, sprinkle on each peach half and dust lightly with ground cinnamon. Serves 4.

bananas with yoghurt

Slice 4–5 large bananas at an angle to give longish ovals of banana about 4 cm (1 1/2 in) thick. Arrange in overlapping circles in a round, shallow dish. Mix 60 ml (2 fl oz/1/4 cup) fresh orange juice with 3 teaspoons orange flower water and sprinkle over the banana. Mix 250 g (9 oz/1 cup) thick Greek-style yoghurt with 2 tablespoons honey and pile in the centre of the banana. Lightly roast and chop 60 g (2 1/4 oz/1/2 cup) walnut pieces and sprinkle over the yoghurt and bananas. Drizzle 1 tablespoon thick honey over the walnuts. Serves 4.

watermelon with rosewater and mint

briouats with
dates and figs . . . . makes 18

FOR THESE PASTRIES, USE THE SOFTER DESSERT FIGS, OR, IF ONLY DRIED FIGS ARE AVAILABLE, PICK OUT THE
SOFTER ONES. IF DESIRED, ONLY DATES MAY BE USED WITH THE ALMONDS, BUT THE COMBINATION OF FRUITS
MAKES THESE ALL THE MORE ENJOYABLE.

smen or butter	125 g (4½ oz/½ cup), melted
blanched almonds	150 g (5½ oz/1 cup)
dates	80 g (2¾ oz/½ cup)
	chopped and pitted
dessert figs (soft, dried figs)	80 g (2¾ oz/½ cup) chopped
orange flower water	1 tablespoon
filo pastry	12–14 sheets
icing (confectioners') sugar	to serve

In a small frying pan, warm 1 tablespoon of the smen, add the almonds and cook over medium heat, stirring often, until golden. Tip immediately into a food processor, along with the smen in the pan. When the almonds are cool, process until finely chopped, then add the dates, figs and orange flower water and process to a thick paste, scraping down the side of the bowl as necessary. Turn out onto the work surface, rub your hands with a little of the smen and gather the paste into a ball. Roll into a sausage 23 cm (9 in) long and cut it into 18 equal pieces. Roll each piece into a cigar shape 10 cm (4 in) long. Place on a sheet of baking paper and set aside.

Count out 12 sheets of filo pastry (if the pastry is shorter than 39 cm (15½ in) in length, you will need extra sheets). Stack the filo on a cutting surface and, with a ruler and sharp knife, measure and cut across the width through the stack to give strips 13 cm (5 in) wide and about 28–30 cm (11–12 in) long. Stack the cut filo in the folds of a dry tea towel or cover with plastic wrap to prevent it from drying out.

Place a strip of pastry with the narrow end nearest you and brush with the warm, melted smen. Top with another strip of pastry and brush with melted smen. Put the shaped filling 1 cm (½ in) from the base and about 1.5 cm (⅝ in) from the sides of the strip. Fold the end of the filo over the filling, fold in the sides and brush the side folds with smen. Roll to the end and place seam side down on a greased baking tray. Repeat with the remaining ingredients. Preheat the oven to 180°C (350°F/Gas 4) after the briouats are completed to keep the kitchen cool while shaping.

Brush the tops of the briouats lightly with smen and bake in the preheated oven for 20 minutes, or until lightly golden. Sift icing sugar over them while still hot. When cool, store in a sealed container. The rolls keep for two days stored at room temperature.

Roll each piece of the paste into a short cigar shape.

Put the filling at the bottom of the strip and fold the filo over it.

mint tea

Mint grows abundantly in Morocco, and was favoured as a tisane in the past, but with the opportune introduction of green tea in the 1850s, Moroccans discovered the two ingredients were made for each other. Spearmint (*Mentha spicata or M. viridis*) is the preferred mint and the preferred tea is green gunpowder, more specifically, Formosan Gunpowder tea.

Put the tea in a warmed teapot, with the amount varying according to the maker's tastes — about 1 tablespoon is usual. Pour in boiling water, leave to brew for a minute or so, then add 1–2 tablespoons sugar and a good handful of well-washed, leafy mint stalks. Brew for 3 minutes. Pour the tea into a tea glass, then return it to the teapot to mix the brew. Pour the tea into tea glasses with a sprig of mint. The mint in the teapot acts as a strainer for the tea leaves.

In Morocco, tea is usually sweetened generously with highly refined loaf sugar; this is shaped in cones about 20 cm (8 in) high, wrapped in purple paper (or plastic), and the amount required is broken off by the tea maker using a special silver hammer. The teapot, of the British shape known as 'Manchester' with a bulbous body and domed lid, is made in silver plate, aluminium or stainless steel. Tea is poured from a height to aerate it, and is sometimes poured from two teapots for maximum effect and aeration — guests are expected to have three glasses. And how do you drink hot tea from a glass? Grip the rim of the glass with the thumb and forefinger of the right hand and sip.

date candies . . . . serves 6–8

THE BERBERS, ESPECIALLY NOMADIC TRIBES, DEPENDED HEAVILY ON THE DATE AS A FOOD. DATES ARE USED WIDELY IN THEIR COOKING, AND ARE MADE INTO SWEETMEATS WITH A RANGE OF INGREDIENTS. THE INCLUSION OF SMEN AND NUTS INCREASES THE ENERGY VALUE OF THIS PARTICULAR SWEETMEAT.

walnut halves	150 g (5½ oz/1½ cups)
sesame seeds	2 tablespoons
smen or ghee	100 g (3½ oz)
pitted dried dates	600 g (1 lb 5 oz), coarsely chopped

Preheat the oven to 180°C (350°F/Gas 4) and line the base of an 18 cm (7 in) square tin with baking paper. Spread the walnuts on a baking tray and bake for 5 minutes, or until lightly roasted. Chop coarsely. Bake the sesame seeds on a tray until golden.

Melt the smen or ghee in a large heavy-based saucepan and cook the dates, covered, over low heat for about 10 minutes, stirring often, until the dates soften. Using the back of a spoon dipped in cold water, spread half the dates over the base of the prepared tin. Scatter the walnuts on top and press into the dates. Spread the remaining dates over the walnuts. Smooth the surface with wet fingers and press down firmly.

Sprinkle with the sesame seeds and press lightly into the dates. When cool, remove the set mixture from the tin and cut into small diamonds to serve.

To make smen (clarified butter), cut 250 g (9 oz) salted or unsalted butter into pieces and put in a small, heavy-based saucepan over low heat, using a heat diffuser if necessary to prevent the butter from spitting. Simmer very gently for 25 minutes, or until the milk solids brown very lightly. Pour the hot butter through a muslin-lined strainer set over a bowl. The clear oil is the smen. It will have a slightly nutty taste. A herbed smen is also made by putting some za'atar (a wild thyme-like herb) and salt into the strainer and pouring the hot butter oil through this to flavour it. Store smen in a sealed jar in the refrigerator. Ghee is a good substitute.

rice pudding with raisins . . . . serves 8

THIS IS SERVED IN A COMMUNAL DISH IN MOROCCAN HOUSEHOLDS, AND EATEN WITH A SPOON. THE TOPPING CAN VARY — USUALLY DABS OF BUTTER ARE PLACED ON THE WARM PUDDING, BUT CHOPPED TOASTED ALMONDS, OR RAISINS AND HONEY AS IN THE RECIPE BELOW, GIVE IT A FESTIVE AIR.

short-grain rice	110 g (3¾ oz/½ cup)
milk	1.125 litres (39 fl oz/4½ cups)
sugar	55 g (2 oz/¼ cup)
ground almonds	55 g (2 oz/½ cup)
cornflour (cornstarch)	2 tablespoons
almond extract	¼ teaspoon
orange flower water	2 tablespoons
raisins	2 tablespoons
honey	2 tablespoons

Put the rice in a large heavy-based saucepan with a pinch of salt and 250 ml (9 fl oz/1 cup) water. Cook over medium heat for 5 minutes, stirring occasionally, until the water has been absorbed.

Set aside 125 ml (4 fl oz/½ cup) of the milk. Stir 250 ml (9 fl oz/ 1 cup) of the remaining milk into the rice, bring to a simmer, and when the rice has absorbed the milk, add another 250 ml (9 fl oz/ 1 cup) milk. Continue to cook the rice until all the milk has been added, ensuring each addition of milk is absorbed before adding the next. (Adding the milk gradually helps prevent the milk from boiling over.) The rice should be very soft in 30 minutes, with the final addition of milk barely absorbed.

Mix the sugar with the ground almonds and break up any lumps. Stir into the rice mixture and simmer gently for 2–3 minutes. Mix the cornflour with the reserved milk and stir into the rice. When thickened, boil gently for 2 minutes. Remove the pan from the heat and stir in the almond extract and 1½ tablespoons of the orange flower water. Stir the pudding occasionally to cool it a little.

Meanwhile, steep the raisins in the remaining 2 teaspoons of orange flower water for 15 minutes. Pour the pudding into a serving bowl and when a slight skin forms on the top, sprinkle with the soaked raisins and drizzle with the honey. Cool completely before serving in individual bowls.

Cook the rice, stirring occasionally, until the water is absorbed.

Gradually add the milk to the rice and cook until absorbed.

index

This edition first published in Canada in 2005 by Whitecap Books, 351 Lynn Ave., North Vancouver, British Columbia, Canada, V7J 2C4.

www.whitecap.ca

First published in 2005 by Murdoch Books Pty Limited.

Design concept and design: Vivien Valk
Editor: Justine Harding
Text and recipes: Tess Mallos
Additional recipes: Murdoch Books Test Kitchen
Food editor: Jane Lawson
Photographers: Ashley Mackevicius, Prue Ruscoe and Ian Hofstetter; Martin Brigdale (location)
Stylists: Wendy Berecry, Jane Hann and Katy Holder
Food preparation: Ross Dobson and Georgina Leonard
Production: Monika Paratore

ISBN 1-55285-643-7

Printed by Toppan Printing Hong Kong Co. Ltd. in 2005. PRINTED IN CHINA.

IMPORTANT: Those who might be at risk from the effects of salmonella poisoning (the elderly, pregnant women, young children and those suffering from immune deficiency diseases) should consult their doctor with any concerns about eating raw eggs.

CONVERSION GUIDE: You may find cooking times vary depending on the oven you are using. For fan-forced ovens, as a general rule, set the oven temperature to 20°C (70°F) lower than indicated in the recipe. We have used 20 ml (4 teaspoon) tablespoon measures. If you are using a 15 ml (3 teaspoon) tablespoon, for most recipes the difference will not be noticeable. However, for recipes using baking powder, gelatine, bicarbonate of soda, small amounts of flour and cornflour (cornstarch), add an extra teaspoon for each tablespoon specified.